# Transforming Business with AI:

# Sustainable Innovation and Growth

## Dr. Yashwant Aditya

# Dedication

To My Wife,

My inspiration, my anchor, my heart's true north—

In the tapestry of our lives, you are the golden thread that weaves through every moment, illuminating the ordinary and making the extraordinary possible. Your love has been the ink in my pen, the fire in my soul, and the courage in my convictions.

With each sunrise, your encouragement dawned anew, chasing away the shadows of doubt. In the quiet hours of creation, your faith whispered louder than any inner critic. You've been the silent co-author of every page, your spirit infusing each word with purpose and passion.

Through storms of uncertainty and deserts of writer's block, you were my oasis of calm, my wellspring of inspiration. You celebrated the small victories as if they were epic triumphs and shouldered the weight of setbacks as if they were mere pebbles on our shared path.

This book is a love letter to your unwavering support, a monument to the power of partnership. It stands as proof that behind every dream achieved is a love that believes in it first.

You've been my first reader, my harshest critic, and my most ardent supporter. In you, I've found not just a partner, but a collaborator in life's grandest adventure.

To call this book mine would be a fallacy—it is ours, born from your encouragement and nurtured by your endless love.

For every late night you kept vigil, for every doubt you dispelled, for every moment you chose to believe in us—thank you. This dedication pales in comparison to the novel of gratitude written in my heart.

With boundless love and eternal appreciation,

-- Yashwant

P.S. In every word, in every page, in every chapter—I love you.

# Contents

# Chapter 1:
# Understanding AI and Its Relevance

The business landscape is undergoing a shift fueled by Artificial Intelligence (AI). No longer relegated to the realm of science fiction, AI is rapidly transforming industries, from streamlining operations to creating entirely new revenue streams. But how can businesses harness the power of AI to gain a competitive edge?

This chapter serves as your guide to AI in business. We'll begin by looking into the fundamentals of AI, delving into some of its key components to help you understand how these technologies work together to create intelligent systems that can learn, adapt, and solve complex problems relevant to various business functions.

Next, we'll embark on a historical journey, tracing the evolution of AI in business contexts. From the early days of basic automation to today's sophisticated applications, we'll explore the remarkable progress AI has made in serving businesses.

Understanding the present is crucial for navigating the future. This chapter will equip you with the knowledge to do just that. By leveraging data and charts, we'll clearly show how AI impacts everything from healthcare and finance to retail and manufacturing.

**What Is AI?**

Artificial Intelligence (AI) represents a transformative leap in technology, promising to reshape the business landscape in unprecedented ways.

But what exactly is AI? We are accustomed to it now, but let's examine its technicality. At its core, AI refers to the simulation of human intelligence in machines designed to think and learn like humans. These intelligent systems can perform tasks that typically require human intelligence, such as recognizing speech, making decisions, and identifying patterns.

**Historical Evolution of AI in Business**

The journey of AI from theoretical concepts to practical business applications has been long and eventful. Understanding this evolution provides valuable insights into how AI has become pivotal in modern business.

**Early Beginnings:**

The roots of AI can be traced back to the mid-20th century when pioneers like Alan Turing began exploring the possibility of machines simulating human intelligence. Turing's work laid the foundation for the field, with his famous Turing Test providing a benchmark for machine intelligence.

**ADD INFOGRAPHIC OF EVOLUTION OF AI FROM 20th**

## Century

**The Advent of Machine Learning:**

The 1980s and 1990s saw a shift towards machine learning, emphasizing systems that could learn from data. During this period, businesses began to adopt AI technologies for specific tasks, such as fraud detection in banking and inventory management in retail. Though rudimentary by today's standards, these applications demonstrated AI's potential to improve efficiency and decision-making processes in business operations.

**The Rise of Big Data and Deep Learning:**

The 21st century ushered in the era of big data, characterized by an explosion of digital information generated by the internet and connected devices. Concurrently, advancements in computing power and deep learning techniques have revolutionized AI capabilities. Businesses began leveraging these advancements to gain deeper insights into customer behavior, optimize supply chains, and enhance product development. Companies like Google and Facebook pioneered using AI to personalize user experiences and drive engagement.

**AI in the Digital Age:**

Today, AI is ubiquitous in business, driving innovation and creating new industry opportunities. As we look ahead, the role of AI in business is poised to expand even further. Emerging trends such as the Internet of Things (IoT), autonomous systems, and edge computing are set to amplify the impact of AI. Businesses that harness these technologies can offer smarter products and services, create more efficient operations, and make data-driven decisions with greater precision.

One of the most exciting prospects is the potential for AI to drive innovation in previously unimaginable ways. For instance, AI-powered design tools can create new products and solutions optimized for performance and cost. In customer experience, AI can provide hyper-personalized interactions, enhancing customer satisfaction and loyalty. Furthermore, AI can help address some of the most pressing global challenges, such as climate change, by optimizing resource use and enabling more sustainable practices.

However, integrating AI in business also presents significant challenges and considerations. Ethical concerns around data privacy, algorithmic bias, and job displacement must be addressed to ensure that AI is used responsibly and equitably. Businesses must also invest in building AI literacy among their workforce and fostering a culture of continuous learning to keep pace with rapid technological advancements.

**Current Trends in AI and Future Projections**

# Transforming Business with AI

## Current Trends in AI and Future Projections

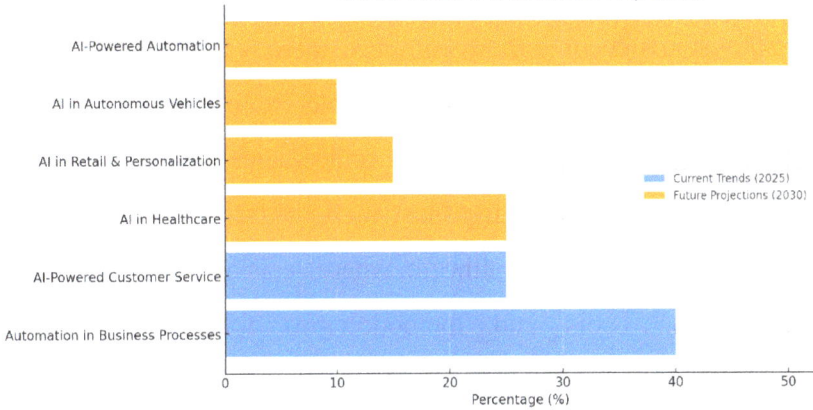

Artificial Intelligence (AI) has evolved from a niche area of computer science into a transformative force reshaping industries and everyday life. As we stand at the forefront of this technological revolution, understanding current trends and future projections is essential for grasping the full scope of AI's impact.

## Current Trends in AI

*Generative AI:*

One of the most prominent trends is the rise of generative AI. Technologies like OpenAI's GPT models and DALL-E have demonstrated AI's ability to create text, images, and music. Generative AI is utilized for everything from content creation and personalized marketing to drug discovery and art. This trend signifies a shift from AI being an analysis tool to creating novel content and solutions.

Dr. Yashwant Aditya

*Explainable AI (XAI):*

As AI systems become more complex, there is a growing demand for explainability. Explainable AI seeks to make AI decision-making processes transparent and understandable to users. This trend is crucial for building trust in AI systems, particularly in sectors like finance and healthcare, where decisions have significant implications. Tools and methodologies for improving the interpretability of AI models are being developed to ensure that stakeholders can understand and trust AI-generated insights.

*Ethics and Fairness in AI:*

Ethical considerations and fairness are becoming central to AI development. There is increasing awareness of the biases embedded in AI models and the need for responsible AI practices. The focus on ethical AI drives the creation of frameworks and guidelines to ensure that AI systems are developed and deployed in equitable and just ways.

## ADD INFOGRAPHIC OF POSSIBLE APPLICATIONS OF AI

**Future Projections**

Looking ahead, the future of AI promises even greater advancements and challenges. AI is expected to continue its rapid development, with several key projections shaping the landscape:

*Ubiquitous AI Integration:*

AI is anticipated to become even more integrated into daily life and business operations. The proliferation of smart devices and the Internet of Things (IoT) will lead to more interconnected AI systems, enhancing personalization and automation in various sectors.

*Advancements in General AI:*

While current AI systems are specialized for specific tasks, future research will likely focus on developing General AI—machines with broad cognitive abilities similar to human intelligence. This leap could revolutionize how AI interacts with the world, but it also raises ethical and safety concerns that must be addressed.

*AI and Human Collaboration:*

The future will see increased collaboration between AI and humans. AI is expected to augment human capabilities rather than replace them, leading to new forms of human-AI collaboration that enhance creativity, decision-making, and problem-solving.

*Regulation and Governance:*

As AI technologies advance, regulatory frameworks will evolve to address emerging ethical and safety issues. Governments and organizations will likely implement more comprehensive regulations to ensure responsible AI development and deployment, balancing innovation with public welfare.

As we look to the future, the continuous development of AI will bring both opportunities and challenges, shaping how we interact with technology and each other. The journey of AI is far from over, and its future promises to be as dynamic and transformative as its present.

*Future Projections of AI Growth:*

The future of AI looks promising, with continuous advancements expected to drive further adoption and innovation across industries.

Businesses are expected to significantly increase their investment in AI technologies. Countries like China and India invest substantially in AI infrastructure and talent development. As AI solutions become more accessible and affordable, SMEs are expected to embrace AI technologies to enhance their competitiveness. Cloud-based AI services and platforms are lowering the barriers to entry, enabling smaller businesses to leverage AI for analytics, customer service, and operational efficiency.

The future will see a greater emphasis on ethical AI and regulatory frameworks. As AI becomes more pervasive, concerns around data privacy, algorithmic bias, and job displacement will prompt stricter regulations and ethical guidelines. Companies must adopt transparent and accountable AI practices to maintain public trust and comply with regulations.

Transforming Business with AI

The transformative potential of AI in business is immense. From its humble beginnings as a theoretical concept to its current status as a driving force of innovation, AI has consistently demonstrated its ability to revolutionize industries and improve businesses' operations. This is your opportunity to unlock a competitive advantage and propel your business towards a brighter, AI-powered future.

## 1. Quick Quiz: AI Fundamentals (Multiple Choice & True/False Questions)

- **What does AI primarily simulate?**
  a) Human emotions
  b) Human intelligence
  c) Physical strength
  d) Random behaviors
- **Which of the following is NOT a component of AI?**
  a) Machine Learning
  b) Deep Learning
  c) Mechanical Engineering
  d) Natural Language Processing
- **True or False:** AI only became useful for businesses in the 21st century.
- **True or False:** The Turing Test was designed to evaluate machine intelligence.

**Answers:**

1. b) Human intelligence
2. c) Mechanical Engineering
3. False
4. True

## 2. Reflection Exercise: AI in Your Industry

- Identify a business sector you're interested in (e.g., healthcare, finance, retail).
- Research and list **three real-world AI applications** in that industry.
- Write a short paragraph on **how AI could transform** this industry in the next 10 years.

## 3. Timeline Challenge: AI's Evolution (Match the events to their correct time period)

- Alan Turing proposes the concept of machine intelligence. *(1940s-50s)*
- Introduction of machine learning and early AI applications. *(1980s-90s)*
- The rise of deep learning and big data-powered AI. *(2000s-2010s)*
- Widespread AI adoption in business operations. *(2020s and beyond)*

## 4. Debate Topic: AI – A Boon or a Threat to Business? *(Group*

*or Solo Activity)*

- Divide into two perspectives: **AI as a growth driver** vs. **AI as a risk factor**
- Consider topics like job displacement, data privacy, and innovation.
- Prepare arguments and counterarguments for a brief discussion or written reflection.

## 5. Hands-On Exploration: AI in Everyday Life *(Mini Research Task)*

- Find **three AI-powered tools or apps** that you use in daily life (e.g., Google Assistant, ChatGPT, Netflix recommendations).
- Describe how AI enhances their functionality.
- Reflect on whether AI's presence in these areas is **helpful or intrusive.**

# Chapter 2:

# Impact of AI on Business, Economics and Innovation

Artificial Intelligence (AI) has emerged as a transformative force in business, reshaping industries and redefining how organizations operate. Its undeniable significance lies in its technological prowess and its profound impact on innovation, strategy formulation, and competitive positioning.

AI fuels innovation by enabling businesses to explore new possibilities and push the achievable boundaries. By automating repetitive tasks, AI frees up human resources for more creative and strategic endeavors. This efficiency allows businesses to streamline operations and allocate resources more effectively.

Its algorithms analyze vast amounts of data at unprecedented speeds, uncovering insights that human analysts might miss. These insights can reveal market trends, customer preferences, and operational inefficiencies, providing a fertile ground for innovation. By leveraging AI for product development and service delivery, businesses can enhance quality, customize offerings to individual needs, and introduce new features that resonate with customers.

**Market competition:**

AI-driven market analysis provides real-time insights into competitors, customer sentiment, and industry trends, helping businesses anticipate shifts in market dynamics and adjust strategies accordingly.

- o Sephora leverages artificial intelligence (AI) to generate dynamic landing pages featuring real-time product descriptions tailored to your specific search queries.
- o Google's at the forefront of AI; they've put that power in your hands with their AI-powered marketing tools on Google Cloud. These tools offer features like marketing analytics, automated bidding, and chatbots, helping you stay ahead of the curve.

**Personalization:**

AI enables personalized marketing campaigns, customer service interactions, and product recommendations based on individual preferences and behaviors, enhancing customer satisfaction and loyalty.

- o Retail giant H&M leverages AI-powered chatbots to provide helpful customer service, offering real-time product information, sizing, and more.
- o Eye-oo, a multi-brand eyewear platform with designer and limited-edition pieces, leverages AI-powered customer service (Tidio) to ensure quality and trust throughout the

buying journey.

## Risk Management:

AI models assess risks more accurately by identifying potential threats and vulnerabilities early, allowing businesses to implement preemptive measures and mitigate adverse impacts.

- o Walmart uses AI and data analysis to predict customer demand, ensuring they have the right amount of stock to avoid overspending on last-minute adjustments or disappointing customers with empty shelves.
- o Keeping your money safe is a priority for PayPal. That's why they leverage cutting-edge AI to analyze massive datasets of transactions. These AI tools can spot unusual patterns and red flags that might indicate fraud, helping to keep your account secure.

## Operational Optimization:

AI optimizes supply chain management, logistics, and inventory control by predicting demand fluctuations, optimizing routes, and minimizing operational costs.

- o UPS has incorporated an AI-based chatbot called UPS Bot to automate back-office tasks such as shipment tracking, customer inquiries, and rate quotes.
- o German logistics giant DHL is a prime example of AI in

action. Their warehouses use autonomous forklifts for increased operational efficiency and enhanced safety standards within their warehouse facilities.

## AI Technologies Explained

Artificial Intelligence (AI) encompasses various technologies that enable machines to mimic human intelligence. Among these, machine learning, deep learning, and natural language processing are some of the most impactful in business. These technologies bring unique capabilities, driving innovation and efficiency across various industries.

## Machine Learning

Machine learning (ML) is a subset of AI that focuses on developing algorithms that allow machines to learn from and make predictions based on data. It involves feeding large amounts of data to algorithms, which adjust and improve their predictions over time.

## How Machines Learn from Data:

Machine learning relies on two primary methods of learning from data: supervised learning and unsupervised learning.

## Supervised Learning:

In supervised learning, the algorithm is trained on a labeled dataset, which means that each training example is paired with an output label. For instance, in a dataset containing emails, each email might be labeled "spam" or "not spam." The algorithm learns to associate certain features of the emails (like specific words or phrases) with these labels and can then predict the labels of new, unseen emails.

**Unsupervised Learning:**

Unsupervised learning involves training algorithms on data without labeled responses. The goal is to identify underlying patterns or structures within the data. Clustering is a common unsupervised learning technique where the algorithm groups similar data points together.

For example, in retail, unsupervised learning can be used to discover natural groupings of products frequently bought together, helping inventory management and marketing strategies.

## ADD INFOGRAPHIC OF PRACTICAL APPLICATION OF AI IN ALL BUSINESSES

**Practical Applications of Machine Learning:**

**Fraud Detection in Finance:**

Banks leverage machine learning to fight fraud. These algorithms analyze your transaction data to learn your spending habits and typical locations. If a transaction deviates significantly from these patterns, like a large overseas purchase, the AI raises a flag for human experts to review. This keeps your money safe while ensuring a smooth experience for legitimate transactions.

**Predictive Maintenance in Manufacturing:**

Machine learning in factories acts like a fortune teller for equipment. Sensors collect data on vibrations, temperature, and more. By analyzing this data, the models can predict when a machine will likely fail, allowing for maintenance before a costly breakdown occurs. This extends equipment life and keeps operations running smoothly.

**Deep Learning**

Deep learning is a specialized branch of machine learning that uses neural networks with multiple layers to analyze complex data. These neural networks are designed to mimic the human brain, enabling them to recognize patterns and make decisions accurately.

**The Use of Neural Networks for Complex Data Analysis:**

Deep learning algorithms, or artificial neural networks, consist of multiple layers of interconnected nodes. Each node processes a portion of the input data and passes the result to the next layer. This layered approach allows the network to learn increasingly abstract data features, making it particularly effective for image and speech recognition tasks.

**Practical Applications of Deep Learning:**

**Medical Imaging in Healthcare:**

Deep learning algorithms analyze medical images like X-rays and

Dr. Yashwant Aditya

MRIs to detect anomalies and diagnose conditions like cancer.

**Autonomous Vehicles in Transportation:**

Self-driving cars use deep learning to process vast amounts of data from sensors and cameras, enabling them to navigate complex environments and make real-time driving decisions.

**Natural Language Processing**

Natural Language Processing (NLP) is a branch of AI that focuses on enabling machines to understand, interpret, and respond to human language. NLP combines computational linguistics with machine learning to process and analyze large amounts of natural language data.NLP technologies are transforming how businesses interact with customers and process information in the following ways:

**Language Translation:**

NLP algorithms power translation services like Google Translate, which can convert text or speech from one language to another in real-time. This capability is invaluable for global businesses communicating with customers and partners across different languages.

**Sentiment Analysis:**

Businesses use sentiment analysis to gauge public opinion and customer sentiment from social media, reviews, and feedback. NLP

18

algorithms analyze text data to determine whether the sentiment expressed is positive, negative, or neutral, helping companies understand customer perceptions and improve their offerings.

**Customer Service:**

Chatbots and virtual assistants powered by NLP handle customer inquiries and provide support around the clock. These systems can understand and respond to customer requests, improving service efficiency and customer satisfaction.

**Practical Applications of NLP:**

**Chatbots in Retail:**

Online retailers deploy NLP-powered chatbots to assist customers with product inquiries, order tracking, and troubleshooting, enhancing the shopping experience and reducing the workload on human support staff.

**Sentiment Analysis in Marketing:**

Marketing teams use NLP tools to analyze customer reviews and social media posts, gaining insights into customer preferences and sentiment toward their products. This information guides marketing strategies and product development.

**Real-World Examples of Companies Successfully Implementing AI**

Dr. Yashwant Aditya

Science fiction is no longer the sole domain of intelligent machines. Artificial intelligence (AI) has permeated the business world, transforming how companies operate and achieve success.

## 1. Amazon: Revolutionizing E-commerce and Logistics

Amazon has leveraged AI to enhance nearly every aspect of its business operations. One of the most notable implementations is the recommendation engine, which uses machine learning algorithms to analyze customer behavior and preferences. This AI-driven system significantly boosts sales by personalizing shopping experiences and suggesting products customers are likelier to purchase.

Amazon uses AI to optimize its supply chain and delivery processes in logistics. The company's fulfillment centers are equipped with robots that work alongside human employees to increase efficiency and reduce costs.

## 2. IBM Watson in Healthcare: Transforming Diagnosis and Treatment

IBM Watson has become a pioneering force in healthcare by assisting doctors in diagnosing and treating patients. One notable application is its use in oncology, where Watson analyzes vast amounts of medical data, including patient records, clinical trials, and scientific literature, to provide evidence-based treatment recommendations. This has led to more accurate diagnoses and personalized treatment plans, improving patient outcomes and reducing the time doctors spend on research.

Memorial Sloan Kettering Cancer Center, one of the leading cancer treatment facilities, has partnered with IBM Watson to enhance its clinical decision-making process. By integrating Watson's AI capabilities, the center has been able to speed up the diagnostic process and offer more effective treatment options tailored to individual patient profiles.

## 3. Netflix: Enhancing Viewer Experience with Personalized Content

Netflix utilizes AI to maintain its competitive edge in the streaming industry. The company's recommendation system is powered by machine learning algorithms that analyze user behavior, preferences, and viewing history to suggest content that aligns with individual tastes. This personalized approach keeps users engaged and reduces churn rates.

Moreover, Netflix employs AI for content creation and acquisition. By analyzing viewing patterns and preferences, Netflix can predict which types of shows and movies will be successful, guiding their investment decisions in original content.

## 4. Tesla: Leading the Autonomous Vehicle Revolution

Thanks to its sophisticated AI systems, Tesla is at the forefront of the autonomous vehicle industry. Tesla vehicles collect data from millions of miles driven by customers, which is then used to improve the AI models that power the self-driving capabilities.

Tesla's continuous data collection and iterative improvement approach have enabled the company to make significant strides in autonomous driving technology. The AI systems enhance safety by reducing human error and improve the overall driving experience by automating mundane tasks like highway driving and parking.

**What this means for the future**

*Power of Personalization*

- A key takeaway from Amazon and Netflix is the power of personalization. AI-driven recommendation systems that tailor experiences to individual preferences can significantly enhance user engagement and drive revenue growth. Companies should invest in AI technologies to understand and anticipate customer needs, providing a more personalized and satisfying experience.

*Data Collection*

- Effective AI implementation relies heavily on access to large volumes of high-quality data. Tesla's success in autonomous driving and IBM Watson's breakthroughs in healthcare both underscore the importance of data collection and analysis.

Businesses must prioritize data management strategies, ensuring they have robust systems to gather, process, and analyze data.

*Collaboration Between Humans and AI*

- AI should be viewed as a tool that augments human capabilities rather than replacing them. Amazon's use of robots in fulfillment centers and IBM Watson's role in assisting doctors highlight the synergy between humans and AI. Organizations should focus on integrating AI in ways that complement and enhance human skills, leading to more efficient and effective outcomes.

*Strategic Investment in AI*

- Investing in AI requires a strategic approach, focusing on areas where AI can deliver the most value. Netflix's investment in AI for content recommendation and creation shows the importance of aligning AI initiatives with core business objectives. Businesses should identify key areas where AI can drive significant improvements and allocate resources accordingly.

**AI is a technological advancement and a strategic imperative for businesses seeking to innovate, thrive in competitive markets, and sustain long-term growth. By harnessing the**

Dr. Yashwant Aditya

power of AI to drive innovation and curate strategy, businesses can unlock new opportunities, optimize performance, and deliver exceptional value to customers in an increasingly digital and interconnected world.

# Exercises & Practical Activities

1. **Case Study Analysis:**
   - Research an AI-driven company (e.g., Amazon, Netflix, or PayPal).
   - Identify how AI helps in business decision-making, personalization, or risk management.
   - Summarize your findings in a short report (200-300 words).
2. **AI in Your Industry:**
   - Think of a business or industry you are familiar with (e.g., retail, healthcare, finance).
   - How could AI be applied to improve operations in this industry?
   - Write a short paragraph outlining a potential AI-driven solution.
3. **Ethical Debate:**
   - AI can optimize business operations but may also lead to job displacement.
   - Do you think the benefits of AI outweigh the risks?
   - Write a brief argument supporting or opposing AI's growing influence in business.
4. **Create Your Own AI Business Idea:**
   - If you had to launch a startup that uses AI, what would it do?
   - Describe your AI-powered product or service and explain how it would solve a problem.
5. **Discussion Prompt:**

- "AI is revolutionizing innovation and competition. How do you see AI shaping the future of small businesses compared to large corporations?"
- Share your thoughts in a group discussion or write a response.

# Chapter 3:

# AI integration in the Digital Transformation Strategy for Sustainable Growth

*"Business leaders are excited by the promise of this technology, but they express key concerns about safely integrating it into their organizations. There are worries about vulnerabilities stemming from inaccuracies and misinformation, human error, and internal and external data breaches."*

*- The Harris Poll, published by Insight Enterprises*

Generative AI rapidly reshapes our world, impacting everything from communication to daily work. The question isn't if AI will affect your business but when and how. The good news, however, is that you can take proactive steps to ensure your organization thrives in this AI-powered future. In this chapter, we shall discuss assessing if your organization is ready for AI implementation, its benefits, and how to strategically implement tools to ensure your company benefits the most from AI.

**ADD INFOGRAPHIC OF MAJOR BENEFITS OF AI FOR SUSTAINABLE BUSNESS**

**Assessing your company's readiness for AI:**

1. Understand Business Needs and Objectives

Clearly articulate what you aim to achieve with AI (e.g., process automation, customer insights, predictive analytics) and list potential AI applications relevant to your business, such as chatbots for customer service, recommendation systems, predictive maintenance, or fraud detection.

2. Evaluate Data Readiness
   a. *Data quality*

Any exploration of AI readiness needs to begin with the technology itself. Machine learning, a powerful subset of AI, relies solely on the data it's trained on and the algorithms it uses. High-quality data and well-defined, tested algorithms are the cornerstones of successful AI implementation.

Machine learning thrives on large volumes of clean data. AI models become adept at identifying meaningful relationships and patterns within this data. These patterns then become the foundation for generating knowledge and making intelligent decisions. The quality of the data directly impacts the quality of the insights – the cleaner the data, the more reliable and valuable the business decisions informed by AI will be.

Good data empowers AI models to deliver expert-level insights and make reliable, even autonomous, choices. However, the converse is also true. Inaccurate, incomplete, or insufficient data leads to skewed machine learning. Think of it as feeding a computer with false impressions. Poor data quality misleads the machines and businesses relying on them.

While "big data" holds merit, simply amassing vast amounts of information isn't the answer. The key lies in having the right data – relevant, comprehensive, and covers all potential use cases for your AI implementation.

## b. Data accessibility

Creating an AI-ready infrastructure goes beyond simply acquiring new hardware. Often, it involves transitioning to the immense data storage capabilities offered by cloud services. A critical element here is establishing a single source of truth – a centralized location for all your company's data.

Database technologies like data lakes and lakehouses provide the structure to achieve this. They combine your data into a single pool, offering data scientists the necessary flexibility. Features like query tools, format adaptability, and access to metadata empower them to work with various AI models. For instance, the raw format of data lakehouses allows them to integrate any model they choose seamlessly.

Centralizing data requires an organization-wide integration engine.

This engine, proper planning, engineering resources, and a scalable infrastructure ensure all your data is seamlessly combined. As your business grows and generates new data, the infrastructure should adapt to accommodate the influx effortlessly.

Real-time data processing is also crucial. We can assess your existing technology and provide a roadmap and the necessary engineering resources to help you build this integrated, AI-ready system. This will position your organization to leverage the power of AI effectively.

3. Assessing technical infrastructure

Artificial intelligence is a powerful tool, but it's also a data-hungry one. The success of your AI investments hinges directly on your ability to store and process massive datasets. Simply put, the more complex your data is, the more storage and computational power you'll require.

For organizations embracing AI, cloud migration is practically a necessity. If any significant portion of your IT infrastructure remains on-premise, now's the time for a critical evaluation. Can your current systems handle the demands of your AI readiness strategy?

Here's what a robust AI-ready infrastructure should provide:

a. *Scalable Storage:*

Your storage capacity should seamlessly expand or contract as your data needs evolve.

### b. High-Performance Computing:

Training AI models efficiently on your data requires significant computational power.

### c. Secure Data Access:

Data locality and durability are crucial for ensuring secure and reliable access to your information.

### d. Flexible Architecture:

Your infrastructure needs to be adaptable to handle ever-growing and diversifying datasets. In short, implementing and leveraging AI tools requires a robust technical foundation.

4. Evaluate Workforce Readiness

### a. Education and Culture:

While the technical aspects of AI implementation are important, true AI readiness goes beyond technology. Two crucial pillars are education and fostering a data-driven culture within your organization. Getting these right is often more challenging and time-consuming than the technical hurdles.

### b. Education Combats Fear:

At all levels of your organization, education is essential. When confronted with an unknown capability, fear and anxiety are natural reactions. This can be true for senior managers worried about job security or factory workers concerned about being replaced. However, proper training targeted to specific roles can significantly reduce these anxieties. Basic explanations are not enough, nor are overly technical deep dives. The key is providing relevant training that empowers employees to understand how AI can benefit their roles and the organization.

5. Building a Data-Driven Culture:

AI thrives on data, so fostering a culture that values and understands data is crucial. Encourage collaboration between IT, data science, and business teams. This collaboration ensures everyone is working towards the same goal and that data is used effectively throughout the AI journey.

Employee skill readiness assessments provide valuable insights for management. These assessments help determine the level of investment needed to upskill the workforce to meet the demands of AI integration. Additionally, they can identify employees whose skillsets might be less compatible with AI, allowing for proactive redeployment efforts within the organization.

6. Assessing financial readiness

The allure of AI can be undeniable, but organizations must confront the financial realities before diving in. While AI's disruptive potential and implementation challenges are well-known, the initial investment can be significant. Acquiring an AI solution specifically designed for your business needs can be expensive, and the costs don't stop there. Installation, configuration, and employee training all add to the initial outlay.

Leaders should conduct a thorough financial readiness assessment to ensure they're making sound financial decisions. This assessment helps determine if the potential benefits of AI outweigh the costs. Key considerations include the price of the chosen AI solution, the implementation expenses like installation and training, the ongoing maintenance required to keep the system running smoothly, and the potential talent acquisition costs associated with hiring data scientists and other specialists to support and manage the AI. By carefully weighing these financial aspects upfront, organizations can ensure their foray into AI is strategically sound and fiscally responsible.

Handy Tools for Evaluation:

- ETL (Extract, Transform, Load) Tools

    o **Apache NiFi**: Manages data flow in a scalable and flexible manner.

- o **Talend**: Provides a comprehensive suite for data integration and management.
- o **Informatica:** Offers robust solutions for data integration and quality assessment.
- IT Infrastructure Monitoring Tools
  - o **Nagios**: Monitors system performance and availability.
  - o **Zabbix**: Provides detailed insights into network, server, and application performance.
  - o **SolarWinds**: Offers comprehensive monitoring solutions for IT infrastructure.
- Compliance Tools
  - o **OneTrust**: Helps manage privacy and compliance requirements.
  - o **TrustArc:** Provides solutions for data privacy management and compliance.
- Project Management Tools
  - o **Jira:** Tracks project progress and manages tasks.
  - o **Trello:** Provides a visual way to organize projects and tasks.
  - o **Asana:** Helps manage project timelines and collaboration.
- RFP Tools

- o **RFP360:** Streamlines the request for proposal process, making comparing and selecting vendors easier.

**Key Areas of AI implementation**

1. Data analytics

AI transforms raw data into actionable insights, empowering businesses to make informed decisions and achieve strategic goals.

2. Operations and Supply Chain

AI can optimize operations and streamline supply chain processes, leading to cost savings and increased efficiency.

3. Personalization of marketing campaigns

AI analyzes customer data to personalize marketing campaigns, ensuring messages target specific buying preferences and behaviors. This data-driven approach leads to more relevant and effective campaigns.

4. Risk assessment

AI can help better assess business and financial risks.

5. Product Development

AI can accelerate product development cycles and improve innovation.

6. Generative Design:

Use AI to create innovative design solutions.

7. Quality Control:

Implement AI for real-time quality inspection and defect detection.

8. Sustainability management

AI empowers businesses to identify inefficiencies and optimize resource utilization, fostering a more sustainable approach to daily operations.

**Creating an Efficient AI strategy**

Creating a successful AI strategy requires careful planning, clear vision, and cross-functional collaboration. This chapter will delve into the steps to create an AI strategy and the importance of building a robust, cross-functional AI team. This roadmap will guide your organization from vision setting to execution, ensuring a strategic and effective AI implementation. To stay ahead of the curve and unlock the innovation potential, it's crucial to explore strategically integrating AI into your business today.

1. Define your objectives:

Before launching any major business initiative, including AI implementation, it's critical to establish clear and well-defined objectives. What do you hope to achieve with AI? Are you looking to streamline processes, elevate customer service, develop innovative products, or pursue something entirely different?

A clear vision of your goals will guide your entire AI implementation strategy and serve as a roadmap to measure success. Consider incorporating both short-term and long-term objectives. Short-term goals might focus on immediate improvements such as operational efficiency, cost reduction, or enhanced customer satisfaction. Long-term objectives could be about gaining a competitive edge, fostering a culture of innovation, or even transforming your entire business model.

To ensure your goals are actionable and measurable, remember the SMART framework: Specific, Measurable, Achievable, Relevant, and Time-bound. This framework will help you define goals that are clear, attainable, and directly aligned with your overall AI strategy.

2. Asses and adapt

While the AI landscape constantly evolves, rushing into implementation isn't always the best strategy. AI initiatives often require significant financial investment and resource allocation. Therefore, assessing your organization's readiness is crucial before taking the leap. Are your infrastructure, talent, and budget aligned to support a successful AI implementation?

However, delaying action can also leave you behind. The key is to find the right balance. Here's how:

- o Assess Readiness:

Evaluate your organization's current state. Do you have the necessary resources and infrastructure to support AI integration?

- o Embrace Agility:

The world of AI is fast-paced. Continuously monitor developments in AI technologies and adapt your strategy based on new insights and emerging opportunities. This agility will ensure you capitalize on the ever-evolving landscape of AI.

Following these steps can create a dynamic and powerful roadmap for integrating AI into your organization. This roadmap will empower your business to seize the opportunities presented by the exciting world of artificial intelligence and stay ahead of the curve.

3. Create a roadmap

Don't rush into a full-blown AI implementation. Instead, craft a roadmap that outlines a phased approach. This roadmap should break down your AI journey into stages: pilot projects, scaling, and, ultimately, full deployment. Each phase should have assigned timelines, resources, and clear ownership to ensure smooth execution. Prioritize projects that will deliver quick wins and demonstrate the value of AI to your business. Focus on addressing practical needs where AI can make a tangible difference and choose projects that leverage existing data. This phased approach, coupled with a focus on early wins, will build momentum, secure stakeholder buy-in, and ultimately guide your organization toward a successful AI transformation.

## Building a cross-functional team

What is a cross-functional team?

Cross-functional teams are like all-star teams. They bring together people from different company areas with different skills to work on a project. This way, everyone's ideas can be heard, and they can all learn from each other to achieve a common goal.

The main difference between a cross-functional team and a new department is this: on a cross-functional team, people still have their regular jobs and report to their usual managers. They come together for a specific project to share their skills and ideas. People are permanently assigned to work together under a new manager in a new department.

Benefits of a cross-functional team

- Increase in employee engagement.

Cross-functional teams can be a powerful tool for boosting employee engagement. This is because these teams inherently foster a sense of shared purpose. Unlike traditional departmental structures, where employees might feel isolated or unsure of the bigger picture, cross-functional teams bring together individuals from various departments to work towards a common goal. This collaborative approach creates a sense of unity and allows team members to see how their contributions directly impact the project. Feeling part of something bigger and having a tangible impact on the outcome can be a major motivator, leading to increased employee engagement and satisfaction.

- Production of quality work

Cross-functional teams are the antithesis of the monotonous, departmental grind. They allow individuals to ditch routine tasks and delve into projects with variety and challenge. Imagine a sandbox brimming with diverse skills and knowledge – that's the playground a cross-functional team creates!

While specific team members have their areas of expertise, the collaborative environment fosters an "innovation sandbox" where everyone can experiment and contribute ideas. This melting pot of perspectives ignites creative sparks, leading to solutions that might never have emerged from a single department. So, ditch the silo mentality and embrace the power of cross-functional teams to watch your creativity flourish!

- Promotes a Culture of Innovation

Unlocking the true potential of AI requires a multi-pronged approach. Cross-functional teams are a powerful starting point.

Dr. Yashwant Aditya

Bringing together individuals with diverse expertise and backgrounds creates a dynamic environment where experimentation and innovation are naturally encouraged. Team members from different departments can challenge assumptions, offer fresh perspectives, and explore uncharted territories. This "collision" of ideas fosters a culture where "what if" questions are tolerated and actively encouraged. Calculated risks are seen as opportunities for growth, and even unsuccessful experiments offer valuable learnings that can inform future iterations.

However, fostering a culture of innovation goes beyond simply assembling a diverse team. Recognition is a powerful motivator. Publicly acknowledge and reward creative ideas, even if they haven't yielded a breakthrough. This reinforces the value of innovative thinking and inspires others to step outside their comfort zones. Additionally, consider hosting innovative workshops and hackathons. These events provide dedicated time and space for teams to brainstorm, experiment, and develop creative solutions to specific challenges. The collaborative atmosphere and potential for recognition can ignite a spark of inspiration, leading to groundbreaking solutions that might not have emerged from a single department working in isolation.

By combining the power of cross-functional teams with a culture that celebrates experimentation and recognizes both innovative ideas and successful AI projects, you'll empower your team to push boundaries and unlock the true potential of artificial intelligence within your organization.

**How to build a cross-functional team**

- Cultivate Communication and Collaboration

To cultivate a thriving environment for AI implementation, fostering collaboration across departments is crucial. Imagine a bridge connecting IT, operations, marketing, and customer service – that's the kind of collaboration you want to build. This cross-departmental approach ensures everyone can sit at the table and contribute their unique expertise. To streamline this collaboration, establish regular communication channels. Think of weekly meetings, team chats, or project management platforms. These tools facilitate information sharing, keeping everyone on the same page and ensuring a smooth and successful AI integration process.

- Assign roles and responsibilities.

Assembling your team is just the first step. To ensure smooth sailing, clearly define roles and responsibilities. Who will lead and keep things on track? Who owns which tasks and deliverables? How will everyone communicate and collaborate internally and with other departments involved in the project? Establish a decision-making process, whether democratic voting, a leader's call, or a hybrid approach. Don't forget about conflict resolution – having a clear plan for addressing disagreements constructively minimizes roadblocks and keeps the project on schedule. By mapping out these details, you'll empower your team members, avoid confusion, and foster accountability, setting the stage for a successful cross-functional collaboration.

- Strengthen your leadership capabilities.

To ensure a thriving cross-functional team, prioritize strong leadership. Appoint a dedicated leader from each department to champion your collaborative efforts. These champions will oversee the entire process, from establishing clear policies and procedures for collaboration (ensuring everyone's on the same page) to crafting overarching goals and action plans for each initiative. This joint leadership approach ensures all teams are aligned.

Team leads become internal champions within their departments, communicating the overall plan and how each member contributes to the broader initiative. Motivating them for the initial investment is crucial, and highlighting the long-term benefits (we'll discuss that later) can be a big help. Finally, team leads act as mediators during conflicts, fostering open communication to reach consensus. When an impasse is reached, they may also be empowered to make final decisions to keep the project on track. Strong leadership from the start will equip your cross-functional team to navigate challenges and foster a collaborative culture within your organization.

- Invest in Training and Development

Building strong cross-functional teams for AI initiatives requires investing in your workforce's knowledge.

Implement training programs that equip employees from various departments with foundational AI knowledge. This can be achieved through a Learning Management System (LMS) within your company, offering courses and resources tailored to different roles.

Furthermore, fosters a culture of lifelong learning by encouraging employees to pursue professional development opportunities. Partner with platforms like Coursera for Business, Udacity, or edX to provide access to a vast library of AI courses and certifications. By empowering your team to continuously learn and develop their AI skills, you'll create a more informed and adaptable workforce prepared to leverage the power of AI for your organization's success.

- Leverage External Expertise

To build a robust cross-functional team for your AI endeavors, look beyond your walls and actively engage with the broader AI ecosystem. Collaborate with AI startups, research institutions, and consulting firms. These partnerships can inject fresh perspectives, cutting-edge solutions, and specialized expertise into your team. Moreover, actively participate in AI conferences, webinars, and online forums. These events provide invaluable opportunities to

Dr. Yashwant Aditya

network with industry leaders, stay updated on the latest trends and best practices, and discover innovative approaches that can be adapted for your projects. Use platforms like Kaggle for competitions and collaboration with data science experts.

By fostering a collaborative spirit and actively engaging with the external AI ecosystem, your cross-functional team will gain a broader perspective, access to a wider range of knowledge, and the ability to stay ahead of the curve in this rapidly evolving field. This strengthens your team's ability to tackle complex challenges and deliver impactful AI solutions within your organization.

- Ensure Ethical AI Practices

Develop and enforce a comprehensive set of ethical guidelines that govern AI development and usage throughout your organization. This framework should emphasize transparency, ensuring AI decisions are clear and understandable; fairness, mitigating any potential bias in AI algorithms; and accountability, establishing clear ownership and responsibility for AI outcomes. By prioritizing these core principles, you can foster trust with stakeholders and ensure your AI initiatives have a positive and responsible impact.

AI's Role in Promoting Sustainability

- Enhancing Environmental Sustainability

Artificial intelligence has emerged as a powerful tool in the quest

44

for environmental sustainability, offering innovative solutions to some of the most pressing ecological challenges. One significant area where AI is making a substantial impact is in climate change mitigation. AI algorithms can analyze vast amounts of data from satellites, weather stations, and climate models to predict environmental changes and monitor greenhouse gas emissions. By providing accurate and timely insights, AI enables policymakers and organizations to implement effective strategies for reducing carbon footprints and enhancing climate resilience.

- Supporting Biodiversity and Conservation Efforts

AI's capabilities extend to biodiversity conservation and wildlife protection, which aids in monitoring and preserving ecosystems. AI-powered drones and remote sensing technologies can track wildlife populations, detect illegal activities like poaching and deforestation, and monitor habitat changes with unprecedented accuracy. Machine learning algorithms analyze this data to identify patterns and predict potential threats, allowing conservationists to take proactive measures. For instance, AI can help map critical habitats and migration routes, ensuring that conservation efforts are targeted and effective.

- Advancing Social Sustainability

AI's contribution to sustainability is not limited to the environment;

Dr. Yashwant Aditya

it also plays a pivotal role in promoting social sustainability. In healthcare, AI-driven technologies enhance disease detection, diagnosis, and treatment, improving public health outcomes and reducing healthcare disparities. For instance, AI algorithms can analyze medical images and patient data to identify diseases at an early stage, enabling timely interventions. AI-powered health monitoring devices and telemedicine platforms increase access to healthcare services, particularly in underserved and remote areas, thus promoting health equity.

Artificial intelligence has tremendous potential in promoting sustainability by offering innovative solutions to environmental and social challenges. By enhancing climate change mitigation, optimizing resource use, supporting biodiversity conservation, advancing healthcare, and fostering sustainable urban development, AI contributes to a more sustainable and equitable world.

**By carefully assessing your organization's readiness and setting clear objectives, you can identify areas where AI can deliver the most impact. Developing a well-defined AI strategy and assembling a skilled cross-functional team are crucial for successful implementation.**

# Activity: AI Readiness Self-Assessment & Action Plan

### Step 1: AI Readiness Scorecard (Self-Assessment)

Answer the following questions to evaluate your organization's preparedness for AI adoption.

**Business Needs & Objectives:**

1. Have you clearly defined what AI should achieve in your organization? (Yes/No)
2. Do you have a list of AI applications that can support your business goals? (Yes/No)

**Data Readiness:**
3. Is your data structured, clean, and comprehensive? (Yes/No)
4. Do you have a centralized data storage system (e.g., data lake or cloud infrastructure)? (Yes/No)
5. Is your organization capable of real-time data processing? (Yes/No)

**Technical Infrastructure:**
6. Does your company have scalable storage solutions? (Yes/No)
7. Do you have sufficient computing power to support AI operations? (Yes/No)
8. Is data security and access control a priority in your organization? (Yes/No)

**Workforce Readiness:**
9. Have employees received training on AI concepts and its impact on their roles? (Yes/No)
10. Is there a culture of data-driven decision-making in your organization? (Yes/No)

**Scoring:**

- **8-10 Yes answers:** Your company is AI-ready and well-positioned for digital transformation.
- **5-7 Yes answers:** Your company has a solid foundation but needs further improvements in key areas.
- **0-4 Yes answers:** Significant preparation is required before AI integration.

## Step 2: AI Integration Action Plan

Based on your self-assessment, outline an action plan to enhance AI readiness. Answer the following prompts:

1. **Biggest AI Opportunity:** What is the most promising AI use case for your business?
2. **Key Gaps Identified:** What are the major barriers to AI implementation in your organization?
3. **First Steps:** What immediate actions can be taken to improve AI readiness?
4. **Workforce Strategy:** How will you ensure employees are comfortable using AI tools?

## Step 3: Group Discussion or Reflection

- If completing this exercise in a group setting, discuss AI readiness challenges and solutions with peers.
- If working individually, write a short reflection (100-200 words) on the most important changes your organization should make to integrate AI successfully.

# Chapter 4: AI-Driven Innovation in Various Industries

## AI-Driven Innovations in Healthcare

Artificial Intelligence (AI) is revolutionizing the healthcare industry by enhancing diagnostic accuracy, personalizing patient care, optimizing operational efficiency, and accelerating the development of new treatments. Integrating AI technologies into healthcare has introduced transformative changes, reshaping how medical professionals deliver care and patients experience healthcare services.

### Improving Patient Outcomes and Operational Efficiency

AI is significantly improving patient outcomes and operational efficiency within healthcare. By leveraging advanced algorithms and vast amounts of data, AI helps in various aspects of healthcare, from diagnostics to personalized medicine and hospital management.

1.    Examples of AI in Diagnostics

One of the most impactful areas where AI is transforming healthcare is diagnostics. AI algorithms, especially those based on deep learning, are being trained to interpret medical images, such as X-rays, MRIs, and CT scans, with remarkable accuracy. For example, Google Health's AI system for breast cancer detection has shown that it can outperform radiologists by reducing false positives and negatives. Similarly, AI tools are being developed to assist in diagnosing conditions such as diabetic retinopathy and skin cancers, providing earlier detection and treatment options that can lead to better patient outcomes.

In addition to image analysis, AI is used to interpret other types of medical data, including pathology slides and genomic information. AI-driven platforms can quickly analyze a patient's genetic data to identify mutations linked to specific diseases, such as cancer or rare genetic disorders. This capability allows for more precise diagnoses and targeted treatment plans tailored to the patient's genetic makeup.

2.      Personalized Medicine and Treatment Plans

AI is paving the way for personalized medicine, which tailors medical treatment to the individual characteristics of each patient. By analyzing large datasets of genetic information, medical histories, lifestyle factors, and treatment outcomes, AI can help identify which treatments are most likely effective for a specific patient.

In oncology, for example, AI algorithms can analyze genetic mutations in a patient's tumor and predict which cancer treatments are most likely to work. This approach improves the efficacy of treatment plans and minimizes the risk of adverse effects by avoiding ineffective therapies. Similarly, AI-driven platforms are being used to manage chronic diseases, such as diabetes and heart disease, by continuously monitoring patient data and providing personalized recommendations for medication, diet, and lifestyle changes.

3.    Hospital Management and Operational Efficiency

Beyond clinical applications, AI is enhancing operational efficiency within healthcare institutions. Hospitals and clinics use AI to optimize various administrative tasks, such as scheduling, billing, and inventory management. Machine learning algorithms can predict patient admissions, optimize staff scheduling, and manage supply chains more effectively, leading to cost savings and improved patient flow.

Natural Language Processing (NLP), a subset of AI, is being utilized to automate documentation and streamline administrative tasks. For example, AI-powered voice recognition tools can transcribe clinical notes, reducing the time healthcare providers spend on paperwork and allowing them to dedicate more time to patient care. This automation also helps reduce human errors, ensuring accurate and up-to-date patient records.

AI-driven predictive analytics tools are also used to enhance

Dr. Yashwant Aditya

hospital management by forecasting patient admissions, optimizing resource allocation, and reducing wait times. For instance, predictive models can help hospitals anticipate periods of high patient volume, allowing them to adjust staffing levels and prepare resources accordingly. This proactive approach helps ensure patients receive timely care and that hospitals operate efficiently.

**Case Study:**

**AI in Medical Diagnostics**

To illustrate the transformative potential of AI in healthcare, let's take a closer look at how AI is revolutionizing medical diagnostics.

**AI in Radiology: Enhancing Accuracy and Efficiency**

Radiology is one of the fields where AI has made significant inroads, particularly in image analysis. Traditional diagnostic processes often rely on the expertise of radiologists to interpret medical images and identify abnormalities. However, this process can be time-consuming, and there is a risk of human error, especially in cases where abnormalities are subtle or rare.

AI algorithms, trained on large datasets of medical images, can now assist radiologists by identifying patterns and anomalies that may indicate disease. For example, AI-powered tools are being used to detect lung nodules in chest CT scans, which can be an early sign of lung cancer. These tools can highlight suspicious areas, allowing radiologists to review them more closely and make more informed decisions.

*Stanford University:*

A notable example is a study conducted by researchers at Stanford University, where an AI model was developed to detect pneumonia from chest X-rays. The AI model outperformed radiologists in identifying pneumonia cases, particularly in cases where the condition was less apparent. By providing an additional layer of analysis, AI helps ensure that no potential diagnosis is overlooked, ultimately leading to better patient outcomes.

**AI in Pathology: Improving Diagnostic Accuracy**

Pathology, the study of disease through examining tissues and body fluids, is another area where AI is making a substantial impact. Traditional pathology relies on manually examining tissue samples under a microscope, which can be subjective and prone to variability between pathologists.

AI algorithms can analyze digital pathology slides and identify abnormal cells or tissue patterns that may indicate disease. For instance, AI tools have been developed to detect prostate cancer in biopsy samples with high accuracy. By providing a second opinion, these tools help pathologists confirm their findings and reduce the likelihood of misdiagnosis.

One of the most promising applications of AI in pathology is the

Dr. Yashwant Aditya

analysis of histopathology images to identify breast cancer subtypes. AI models can be trained to recognize specific patterns associated with different types of breast cancer, enabling more accurate and timely diagnoses. This capability is particularly valuable in settings where access to expert pathologists may be limited.

**ADD INFOGRAPHIC OF HOW AI HELPS INCREASE ACCURACY IN HEALTHCARE**

**AI in Genomics: Unlocking Personalized Medicine**

Genomics is another field where AI drives innovation, particularly in personalized medicine. AI algorithms can analyze vast amounts of genetic data to identify mutations associated with specific diseases, such as cancer or rare genetic disorders. This information can then be used to develop targeted treatment plans tailored to the patient's unique genetic makeup.

For example, AI-driven platforms identify genetic mutations that may make patients more susceptible to certain cancers, such as BRCA1 and BRCA2 mutations associated with breast and ovarian cancer. By identifying these mutations early, healthcare providers can develop personalized screening and prevention strategies, ultimately improving patient outcomes.

AI also predicts how patients will respond to specific treatments based on their genetic profiles. In oncology, this approach is known as precision medicine, where AI algorithms analyze a patient's tumor genetics to determine which therapies are most likely effective. This targeted approach reduces the trial-and-error nature of cancer treatment, improving outcomes and reducing side effects.

**Robot-Assisted Surgery: Precision and Minimally Invasive Procedures**

AI has also revolutionized surgical procedures through robot-assisted surgery, which enhances precision, control, and flexibility during operations. These advanced surgical robots, such as the da Vinci Surgical System, use AI algorithms to translate a surgeon's hand movements into smaller, more precise movements of tiny instruments inside the patient's body. This technology allows for minimally invasive procedures, resulting in smaller incisions, reduced blood loss, quicker recovery times, and less postoperative pain for patients. In addition to these benefits, AI-driven robots can provide real-time feedback and imaging, aiding surgeons in making more informed decisions during complex procedures. Integrating AI in robotic surgery is paving the way for safer, more efficient surgical interventions, further improving patient outcomes.

AI is driving a wave of innovation in healthcare, offering new tools and methodologies that enhance patient care, streamline operations, and accelerate medical research. However, navigating the ethical and practical challenges associated with AI is crucial to fully realize its potential in improving health outcomes worldwide.

Dr. Yashwant Aditya

## AI-Driven Innovations in Finance

Artificial Intelligence (AI) transforms the finance industry by enhancing decision-making, optimizing operations, improving customer experiences, and strengthening security measures. The adoption of AI technologies in finance has introduced a range of innovative solutions that are reshaping how financial institutions operate and how customers interact with financial services.

## Enhancing Decision-Making and Risk Management

AI is significantly enhancing decision-making processes and risk management within the finance industry. By leveraging machine learning algorithms and vast datasets, AI systems can analyze market trends, predict future movements, and assess risk more accurately than traditional methods.

1.      Algorithmic Trading and Investment Strategies

Algorithmic trading is one of the most notable applications of AI in finance. AI-driven trading algorithms analyze vast amounts of market data in real-time to identify patterns and execute trades at optimal times. These algorithms use advanced techniques like machine learning and natural language processing (NLP) to analyze structured data, like historical stock prices, and unstructured data, like news articles and social media posts. This ability to process diverse information sources allows AI algorithms to make more informed trading decisions, leading to higher returns and reduced

56

risk.

For instance, hedge funds and investment firms use AI to develop sophisticated trading strategies that adapt to changing market conditions. These AI-driven strategies can automatically adjust portfolio allocations based on market trends, economic indicators, and other relevant factors, optimizing returns while minimizing risk exposure.

2.  Credit Scoring and Risk Assessment

AI is also transforming the way financial institutions assess credit risk. Traditional credit scoring models rely heavily on historical credit data and may not fully capture a borrower's ability to repay a loan. AI-driven credit scoring models, on the other hand, can analyze a broader range of data points, including transaction histories, social media behavior, and even smartphone usage patterns. By incorporating these alternative data sources, AI models can provide a more comprehensive assessment of a borrower's creditworthiness, particularly for individuals with limited credit histories.

Moreover, AI detects fraudulent activities and identifies potential risks in real time. Machine learning algorithms can analyze transaction data to detect unusual patterns that may indicate fraud, such as large withdrawals, frequent transactions in a short period, or transactions in high-risk locations. By identifying these anomalies quickly, financial institutions can take proactive measures to prevent fraud and minimize losses.

## Improving Customer Experience

AI enhances customer experiences in finance by providing personalized services, improving accessibility, and streamlining processes. Financial institutions are increasingly using AI to deliver tailored products and services that meet each customer's unique needs.

1. Personalized Financial Advice and Wealth Management

AI-powered robo-advisors are becoming popular for providing personalized financial advice and wealth management services. These digital platforms use machine learning algorithms to analyze a client's financial situation, goals, and risk tolerance and create customized investment portfolios. Robo-advisors continuously monitor and adjust these portfolios based on market conditions and the client's changing needs, ensuring that the investment strategy remains aligned with the client's objectives.

In addition to robo-advisors, AI enhances customer service in finance. Chatbots and virtual assistants, powered by NLP and machine learning, can provide instant customer support by answering questions, helping with account management, and providing financial advice. These AI-driven tools improve customer satisfaction by offering quick and accurate responses and reduce the workload on human customer service representatives, allowing them to focus on more complex tasks.

2.    Streamlining Banking Operations

AI streamlines banking operations by automating various administrative tasks and improving process efficiency. For example, AI-driven tools are being used to automate the processing of loan applications, reducing the time it takes to approve a loan from days to minutes. AI can quickly assess a borrower's eligibility and determine the appropriate loan terms by analyzing a wide range of data points, including credit scores, income levels, and employment history.

AI is also being used to enhance fraud detection and prevention in banking. Machine learning algorithms can analyze transaction data in real-time to detect suspicious activities and alert banks to potential fraud. This proactive approach helps financial institutions mitigate risks, protect customer accounts, and maintain trust in their services.

**ADD INFOGRAPHIC OF HOW AI IMPROVES CUSTOMER EXPERIENCE**

**Strengthening Security and Compliance**

Security and compliance are critical areas where AI is making a significant impact in finance. Financial institutions are leveraging AI to enhance cybersecurity measures and ensure compliance with regulatory requirements.

1.   AI-Powered Fraud Detection

AI plays a crucial role in detecting and preventing fraud in the finance industry. Machine learning algorithms can analyze vast amounts of transaction data to identify patterns and anomalies indicating fraudulent activities. For example, AI can detect unusual spending patterns, such as multiple large purchases in a short period or transactions from unusual locations, and flag them for further investigation. This real-time monitoring helps financial institutions respond quickly to potential threats and minimize losses due to fraud.

2.   Regulatory   Compliance   and   Anti-Money Laundering (AML)

Compliance with regulatory requirements, such as anti-money laundering (AML) regulations, is a major challenge for financial institutions. AI is helping to streamline compliance processes by automating the monitoring of transactions and identifying suspicious activities that may indicate money laundering or other illegal activities. AI-driven tools can analyze large volumes of transaction data to detect patterns associated with money laundering, such as structuring transactions to avoid reporting thresholds or conducting transactions with high-risk entities.

By automating these processes, AI helps financial institutions reduce the time and resources required for compliance while ensuring they meet regulatory requirements. This minimizes the risk of regulatory penalties and enhances the institution's reputation and trustworthiness.

### *Case Study: AI in Credit Scoring*

To illustrate the transformative potential of AI in finance, let's take a closer look at how AI is revolutionizing credit scoring.

AI-Enhanced Credit Scoring Models: A New Approach to Risk Assessment

Traditional credit scoring models, such as the FICO score, rely heavily on historical credit data, including payment history, credit utilization, and length of credit history. While these factors provide a snapshot of a borrower's creditworthiness, they may not fully capture the individual's financial behavior or potential to repay a loan. This is particularly true for individuals with limited or no credit history, who may be unfairly penalized by traditional scoring models.

AI-driven credit scoring models are changing the game by incorporating more data points into the assessment process. These models use machine learning algorithms to analyze alternative data sources, such as utility payments, rental history, social media activity, and even mobile phone usage patterns. By considering these additional factors, AI models can provide a more comprehensive and accurate assessment of a borrower's creditworthiness, particularly for individuals with limited credit histories.

*Fintech company*

For example, a study conducted by a leading fintech company found that AI-enhanced credit scoring models could reduce the number of creditworthy individuals denied loans due to insufficient credit history by up to 20%. This expands access to credit for underserved populations and helps financial institutions identify new customer segments and reduce default rates.

AI-driven credit scoring models also have the potential to promote fairness and inclusion in the financial system. Considering a wider range of data points, these models can help reduce biases associated with traditional credit scoring methods and provide a more accurate representation of an individual's financial behavior. However, ensuring that AI-driven credit scoring models are transparent, fair, and accountable is essential. Financial institutions must implement robust governance frameworks to monitor the performance of these models and ensure that they do not inadvertently perpetuate existing biases or create new ones.

AI significantly enhances risk management and customer service within the finance industry by providing more sophisticated tools for detecting fraud, assessing creditworthiness, and delivering personalized financial services.

## The Impact of AI on Fraud Prevention

The implementation of AI in fraud detection has had a profound impact on the finance industry. A study conducted by a leading financial institution found that AI-driven fraud detection systems reduced false positives by 50% and increased the detection rate of fraudulent activities by 30%. This improvement helps financial institutions reduce losses due to fraud and enhances customer trust by providing a more secure and reliable service.

Moreover, AI-powered fraud detection systems can provide real-time insights and recommendations to financial institutions, enabling them to take proactive measures to prevent fraud before it occurs. For instance, AI can identify high-risk transactions and flag them for further review or automatically block transactions meeting certain criteria, such as attempts to purchase stolen credit cards.

## AI-Driven Innovations in Retail

Artificial Intelligence (AI) is revolutionizing the retail industry by enhancing customer experiences, optimizing supply chain operations, and providing retailers with valuable insights into consumer behavior. In this section, we will explore how AI is transforming retail through various applications and look closely at a case study on AI in predictive analytics.

Personalizing Customer Experiences

One of the most significant impacts of AI in retail is its ability to personalize customer experiences. Personalization is a key factor in driving customer loyalty and increasing sales, as consumers are more likely to engage with brands that offer tailored recommendations and experiences based on their preferences and behavior. AI technologies, such as machine learning and natural language processing (NLP), enable retailers to analyze vast amounts of data and gain insights into customer preferences, allowing them to deliver highly personalized experiences.

1.      Customer Segmentation and Targeted Marketing

AI plays a crucial role in customer segmentation, which involves dividing customers into distinct groups based on their behavior, preferences, demographics, and other factors. Traditional segmentation methods often rely on limited data points, such as age and location, and may not fully capture the complexities of customer behavior. AI-driven segmentation, on the other hand, uses machine learning algorithms to analyze a wide range of data sources, including purchase history, browsing behavior, social media activity, and customer feedback.

By using AI for customer segmentation, retailers can create more accurate and dynamic customer profiles, enabling them to deliver targeted marketing campaigns that resonate with each segment. For example, AI can identify high-value customers likely to make repeat purchases and tailor marketing messages to encourage loyalty and increase lifetime value. Similarly, AI can identify customers at risk of churning and provide personalized offers to retain them. This level of personalization not only improves customer satisfaction but also drives higher conversion rates and sales.

2.      Personalized Product Recommendations

AI is also enhancing customer experiences through personalized product recommendations. Recommender systems, powered by machine learning algorithms analyze customer data to suggest products most likely to appeal to each shopper. These algorithms use collaborative filtering, content-based filtering, and deep learning techniques to analyze customer behavior, such as browsing history, purchase history, and product ratings, and make personalized recommendations in real-time.

**Optimizing Supply Chains**

In addition to personalizing customer experiences, AI is pivotal in optimizing retailers' supply chain operations. Efficient supply chain management is critical for retailers to minimize costs, reduce waste, and ensure timely delivery of products to customers. AI technologies, such as machine learning, predictive analytics, and computer vision, are helping retailers optimize inventory management, improve demand forecasting, and streamline logistics.

1.    Inventory Management and Stock Optimization

AI transforms inventory management by giving retailers more accurate and data-driven insights into stock levels and product demand. Traditional inventory management methods rely on historical sales data and manual processes, leading to overstocking, stockouts, and increased carrying costs. AI-driven inventory management systems, on the other hand, use machine learning algorithms to analyze real-time sales data, market trends, and external factors, such as weather and economic conditions, to optimize stock levels.

By using AI effectively for inventory management, retailers can ensure they have the right products in the right quantities at the right time, reducing the risk of overstocking or stockouts. This optimization level helps retailers reduce inventory costs, improve cash flow, and enhance customer satisfaction by ensuring product availability.

2.    Demand Forecasting

Accurate demand forecasting is essential for retailers to make informed inventory, pricing, and promotions decisions. AI is revolutionizing demand forecasting by providing retailers with more accurate and granular insights into future demand. Traditional forecasting methods often rely on historical sales data and may not fully capture consumer behavior and market dynamics complexities. On the other hand, AI-driven demand forecasting uses machine learning algorithms to analyze a wide range of data sources, including sales data, customer behavior, market trends, and external factors, to predict future demand.

For example, AI can analyze historical sales data and identify patterns and seasonality in product demand. It can also analyze external factors, weather, holidays, and economic conditions to provide more accurate demand forecasts.

### 3.    Streamlining Logistics and Delivery

AI is also enhancing supply chain efficiency by streamlining logistics and delivery operations. Retailers increasingly use AI-powered tools to optimize routing, scheduling, and delivery processes, ensuring that products reach customers quickly and efficiently. For example, AI can analyze traffic patterns, weather conditions, and delivery data to optimize delivery routes and reduce transit times. It can also analyze order data to prioritize deliveries and allocate resources more effectively.

*Case Study: AI in Predictive Analytics*

Dr. Yashwant Aditya

To illustrate the transformative potential of AI in retail, let's take a closer look at how retailers use AI in predictive analytics to predict customer behavior and trends.

**AI-Powered Predictive Analytics**

Predictive analytics is a powerful tool that uses data, statistical algorithms, and machine learning techniques to identify the likelihood of future outcomes based on historical data. In the retail industry, predictive analytics is used to gain insights into customer behavior, identify trends, and make data-driven decisions about inventory, pricing, and promotions. AI-powered predictive analytics takes this a step further by providing more accurate and dynamic insights that can be used to personalize customer experiences and optimize operations.

For example, a leading global retailer implemented an AI-driven predictive analytics platform to analyze customer data and predict future purchasing behavior. The platform uses machine learning algorithms to analyze various data sources, including transaction history, browsing behavior, social media activity, and customer feedback. By analyzing this data, the platform can identify patterns and trends in customer behavior, such as which products are likely to be popular in the upcoming season or which customers are likely to make repeat purchases.

**ADD INFOGRAPHIC OF HOW AI HELPS IN
FORECASTING FUTURE**

AI is driving a wave of innovation in the retail industry, offering new tools and methodologies that enhance customer experiences, optimize supply chain operations, and provide valuable insights into consumer behavior. As AI continues to evolve, its role in retail will likely expand, paving the way for a more efficient, personalized, and data-driven retail environment.

## AI-Driven Innovations in Manufacturing

Artificial Intelligence (AI) is revolutionizing the manufacturing industry by enhancing production efficiency, improving quality control, and optimizing operations. Manufacturers can reduce downtime, minimize defects, optimize supply chains, and enhance operational efficiency by leveraging AI technologies. This section explores how AI transforms manufacturing, focusing on predictive maintenance, quality assurance, and production optimization. We will also delve into a case study on AI in predictive maintenance to highlight its practical applications and benefits in manufacturing.

## Increasing Production Efficiency and Quality Control

Manufacturing processes have long relied on traditional methods to maintain efficiency and quality control. However, these methods often involve manual inspections and reactive maintenance, which

Dr. Yashwant Aditya

can lead to operational inefficiencies and increased costs. AI now provides manufacturers with innovative solutions to predict equipment failures, enhance quality assurance, and optimize production processes, thereby revolutionizing the industry.

1. Predictive Maintenance

Predictive maintenance is one of the most impactful applications of AI in manufacturing. It involves using AI algorithms to predict equipment failures before they occur, allowing manufacturers to schedule maintenance activities proactively. This approach helps minimize unplanned downtime, reduce maintenance costs, and extend the lifespan of machinery.

Traditional maintenance strategies, such as reactive maintenance (fixing equipment after failure) and preventive maintenance (scheduled maintenance based on time or usage), are often inefficient and costly. Reactive maintenance leads to unexpected downtime and production losses, while preventive maintenance may result in unnecessary repairs and part replacements. In contrast, predictive maintenance leverages AI to analyze data from sensors and machinery to identify patterns and anomalies that indicate potential equipment failures.

2. Quality Assurance and Defect Detection

AI is also transforming quality assurance in manufacturing by providing more accurate and efficient methods for defect detection and quality control. Traditional quality control methods often rely on manual inspections, which can be time-consuming, labor-intensive, and prone to human error. AI-driven quality assurance solutions, on the other hand, use machine learning algorithms and computer vision technology to automate the inspection process and detect defects with higher accuracy and speed.

Machine learning algorithms can analyze images of products captured by cameras on production lines and identify defects that may not be visible to the human eye. These algorithms can be trained to recognize specific types of defects, such as cracks, scratches, or misalignments, by analyzing large datasets of defect images. Once trained, the algorithms can inspect products in real-time, flagging defective items for removal or rework. This automated approach improves the accuracy of defect detection and reduces the need for manual inspections, increasing overall production efficiency.

In addition to defect detection, AI can optimize quality control processes by analyzing data from various stages of production. For example, AI can identify patterns and correlations between production parameters, such as temperature, pressure, humidity, and product quality. By analyzing these relationships, AI can provide insights into the root causes of defects and recommend adjustments to production processes to improve product quality.

3. Production Optimization

Production optimization is another area where AI is making a significant impact in manufacturing. AI technologies, such as machine learning and predictive analytics, are helping manufacturers optimize production processes by analyzing data from sensors, machines, and production lines to identify inefficiencies and opportunities for improvement.

One of the key applications of AI in production optimization is in process control and optimization. AI algorithms can analyze data from sensors and machines in real-time to monitor production parameters, such as temperature, pressure, and speed, and make adjustments to optimize performance. For example, AI can adjust the speed of a conveyor belt or the temperature of a furnace based on real-time data to ensure optimal production conditions. By continuously monitoring and adjusting production parameters, AI helps manufacturers achieve higher efficiency, reduce waste, and improve product quality.

**AI-Powered Predictive Maintenance**

Similar to bringing many benefits in the retail aspect, predictive maintenance is also proving to be helpful in the manufacturing domain. Proactive maintenance strategy that uses AI algorithms to analyze data from machinery and equipment to predict potential failures before they occur. This approach allows manufacturers to schedule maintenance activities proactively, minimizing unplanned downtime, reducing maintenance costs, and improving overall operational efficiency.

A leading automotive manufacturer implemented an AI-driven predictive maintenance solution to monitor production lines and predict equipment failures. The solution uses machine learning algorithms to analyze data from sensors installed on machines, such as vibration data, temperature readings, and acoustic signals. By analyzing this data, the AI algorithms can identify patterns and anomalies that indicate potential equipment failures, such as increased vibration levels or abnormal temperature fluctuations.

The implementation of AI-driven predictive maintenance has had a profound impact on the manufacturer's operations. By leveraging AI to predict equipment failures, the manufacturer reduced unplanned downtime by 30%, resulting in significant cost savings and increased production efficiency. In addition, the manufacturer was able to extend the lifespan of its machinery by performing targeted maintenance activities at optimal times, reducing the need for costly repairs and replacements.

The AI-driven predictive maintenance solution also helped the manufacturer improve overall product quality by ensuring that machinery operates at peak performance. By identifying potential equipment issues before they escalate, the manufacturer could perform maintenance activities proactively, preventing defects and ensuring consistent product quality.

As AI continues to evolve, its role in predictive maintenance will likely expand, offering new opportunities for manufacturers to enhance operational efficiency and reduce costs. In the future, AI-driven predictive maintenance solutions may incorporate additional data sources, such as data from IoT devices, to provide even more accurate predictions and insights.

**As we stand on the brink of this AI-driven future, it is clear that the opportunities are vast and varied. What was once considered a novelty is now becoming necessary as industries increasingly recognize AI's crucial role in driving innovation and efficiency. Those who understand and harness the power of AI will be well-positioned to lead in their respective fields, shaping the next wave of innovation and setting new standards for excellence. The journey of AI in transforming industries has only just begun, and its potential to redefine business as we know it is limitless.**

## AI in Healthcare Case Study Analysis

Read the following short case study and answer the discussion questions.

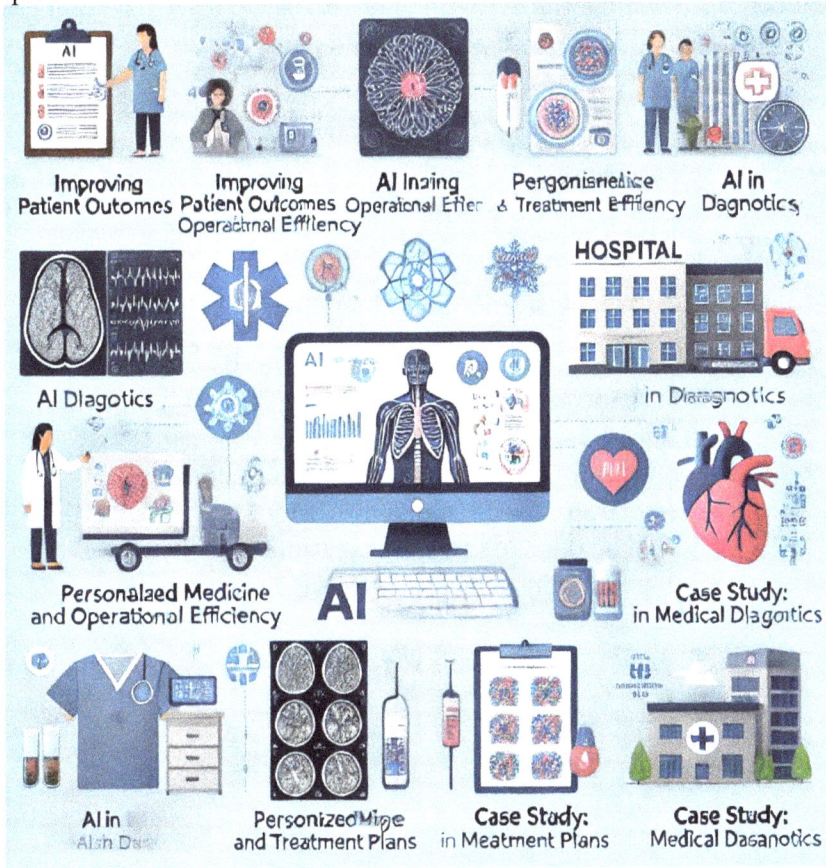

## Case Study: AI in Radiology

Radiology is one of the medical fields where AI has had a significant impact, particularly in diagnostic imaging. Traditional radiologists manually interpret thousands of medical images, which is time-consuming and prone to human error.

Recently, hospitals have started adopting AI-powered diagnostic tools trained on vast datasets of X-rays, MRIs, and CT scans. These AI models analyze medical images within seconds, highlighting potential abnormalities with high accuracy. One notable example is Google Health's AI model, which has been shown to detect breast cancer in mammograms with greater accuracy than human radiologists, reducing false positives and negatives.

Hospitals using AI in radiology report faster diagnosis times, lower costs, and improved patient outcomes. However, some challenges remain, such as ensuring AI model transparency, addressing bias in training data, and integrating AI seamlessly into existing medical workflows.

**Discussion Questions:**

1. What are the key advantages of using AI in radiology for both doctors and patients?
2. What potential challenges might hospitals face when implementing AI-driven diagnostic tools?
3. How can healthcare institutions ensure AI-powered radiology remains ethical, unbiased, and transparent?

# Chapter 5:
# Empowering Diversity and Equity in Artificial Intelligence

## Navigating the Path to Inclusive Innovation

In recent years, Artificial Intelligence (AI) has emerged as a transformative force across various sectors, from healthcare to finance, retail, and beyond. As AI technologies become increasingly integrated into our daily lives, the need to address diversity and equity within this field has never been more pressing. Ensuring that AI development is inclusive and equitable is not just a matter of social justice; it is essential for the technology's effectiveness, fairness, and overall success.

### Significance of Diversity and Equity in AI

Diversity in AI refers to representing different demographic groups—such as race, gender, socioeconomic status, and cultural background—among the people who design, develop, and deploy AI systems. Equity, conversely, involves ensuring fair access to opportunities and resources and addressing disparities that affect different groups within the AI landscape.

The significance of these concepts cannot be overstated. Diverse

Dr. Yashwant Aditya

teams bring varied perspectives and experiences to the table, which can lead to more innovative and creative solutions. In the context of AI, this means developing systems that better reflect the needs and experiences of a broader range of users. For example, AI algorithms trained on data from diverse sources are less likely to perpetuate existing biases or produce outcomes that disadvantage certain groups.

Conversely, lacking diversity can result in AI systems that reinforce stereotypes, exacerbate inequalities, or even cause harm. This is particularly critical when AI is used in decision-making processes that impact people's lives, such as in hiring, law enforcement, and healthcare. If the teams creating these systems lack diverse perspectives, there is a risk that their products will fail to address or even worsen systemic biases.

**Importance of Inclusive Innovation**

Inclusive innovation in AI involves designing and implementing technologies that not only consider but actively incorporate the needs and voices of diverse groups. This approach ensures that AI solutions are equitable and accessible, ultimately leading to more effective and widely accepted technologies.

The importance of inclusive innovation is evident in several ways. Firstly, it helps build trust between technology providers and users. When people see that AI systems are developed with their needs and concerns, they are more likely to embrace and use these technologies. This is crucial for the widespread adoption of AI, as user acceptance and engagement are key to the technology's success.

Secondly, inclusive innovation drives better business outcomes. Companies prioritizing diversity and equity in their AI development processes can tap into new markets and customer segments. By creating products and services that cater to a broader audience, businesses can enhance their market reach and improve their competitive edge.

Moreover, inclusive innovation contributes to social good by addressing and mitigating inequalities. AI systems designed with equity in mind can help reduce disparities in education, healthcare, and economic opportunities. For instance, AI-driven educational tools accessible to all students, regardless of their background, can help bridge educational gaps and promote equal learning opportunities.

As AI continues to evolve and shape various aspects of our lives, prioritizing inclusive innovation is essential for ensuring that these technologies benefit everyone and contribute to a more equitable and just society.

**Understanding Diversity and Equity in AI**

As AI technologies become increasingly embedded in our daily lives, understanding and addressing diversity and equity within this field is crucial. This section delves into what diversity and equity mean in the context of AI, explores the current landscape of diversity within the AI workforce, and examines the disparities and inequities in AI research and applications.

**What is Diversity in the Context of AI?**

Diversity in AI refers to the presence of various demographic groups within the AI ecosystem, including those involved in the development, deployment, and regulation of AI technologies. This encompasses a wide range of factors:

Ethnicity and Race:

Ensuring representation from various racial and ethnic backgrounds.

Gender:

Promoting gender diversity to include women and non-binary individuals in AI roles.

Socioeconomic Status:

Including individuals from different economic backgrounds to avoid a narrow perspective.

Cultural Background:

Incorporating diverse cultural viewpoints to enhance the relevance of AI solutions globally.

Disability:

Ensuring that people with disabilities are represented and their needs are considered. Diversity in AI is not limited to the workforce but includes diversity in the data used to train AI systems. Diverse datasets help create more accurate and equitable AI models by reflecting various experiences and perspectives. This reduces the risk of developing biased or unfair AI systems that may disadvantage certain groups.

**What Constitutes Equity in AI Development and Deployment?**

Equity in AI involves ensuring fair access to opportunities and resources and addressing any systemic barriers that may affect different groups. This includes:

- Providing all individuals, regardless of their background, with the same opportunities to participate in AI-related activities, from education to employment.
- Ensuring that AI systems are designed and deployed in ways that do not unfairly discriminate against or disadvantage any group.
- Making sure that underrepresented groups have access to the tools, education, and funding needed to engage in AI development and research.
- Holding AI systems and their creators accountable for decisions and outcomes ensures transparency in how AI

Dr. Yashwant Aditya

models are developed and how they operate.

**Equity also means addressing historical and structural inequities that have led to underrepresentation in the field. This involves proactive measures to correct these imbalances and create an inclusive environment where everyone can thrive**

**ADD INFOGRAPHIC OF COUNTRIES INVESTING IN USING AI TO IMPROVE THEIR PROCESSES**

**Case Study:**

**IBM's AI Fairness 360 (AIF360)**

**Toolkit and its impact on promoting fairness and inclusivity in AI systems**

IBM's AI Fairness 360 (AIF360) is an open-source toolkit designed to help developers identify and mitigate biases in AI models. Launched in 2018, AIF360 aims to address issues of fairness in machine learning systems and promote ethical AI practices. The toolkit is part of IBM's broader commitment to responsible AI and inclusivity.

**Challenges Addressed**

IBM's AI Fairness 360 (AIF360) toolkit was developed to address the pervasive issue of bias in AI systems, which often reflects the biases inherent in their training data. IBM recognized that biases could lead to unfair and discriminatory outcomes, particularly when

82

AI systems are deployed in sensitive areas such as hiring, lending, law enforcement, and healthcare. The development of AIF360 was driven by several specific challenges IBM faced while creating fair and equitable AI solutions for these industries.

## Origins of Bias in AI Models and AIF360's Focus Areas

a. Historical Biases in Client Data:

*Issue:*

One of the primary challenges IBM faced was that many of its clients' datasets contained historical biases. For example, when working with financial institutions, IBM observed that training data for credit scoring models often reflected discriminatory practices of the past, where minority groups were unfairly denied credit or offered less favorable terms.

*AIF360's Role:*

AIF360 was designed to help detect these historical biases by providing fairness metrics that evaluate model outputs across different demographic groups. By identifying disparities in how different groups are treated, AIF360 enables developers to see where biases might be influencing model behavior.

b. Sampling Bias in Real-World Applications:

*Issue:*

IBM also encountered significant challenges with sampling bias, where the data used to train AI models was not representative of the broader population. For instance, in healthcare, training datasets might be skewed toward data from specific hospitals or regions, leading to models that perform well for those groups but poorly for others.

*AIF360's Role:*

To combat this, AIF360 includes tools for measuring the representativeness of data and adjusting for sampling biases. These tools help ensure that AI models generalize well across diverse populations, reducing the risk of biased outcomes in real-world applications.

c. Label Bias in Supervised Learning:

*Issue:*

Label bias, where the labels in training data reflect subjective human judgments or societal stereotypes, posed another challenge. For example, in predictive policing, crime data labels may be biased due to over-policing in certain communities, which skews AI model predictions.

*AIF360's Role:*

AIF360 provides methods to audit datasets for label bias and offers strategies to mitigate its effects. This includes reweighting techniques and adversarial debiasing methods that adjust model training to minimize the impact of biased labels.

**Consequences of Biased AI Models in IBM's Experience**

a. Discrimination in Decision-Making:

*Impact:*

IBM found that biased AI models could lead to discriminatory decision-making processes.

*AIF360's Contribution:*

By incorporating AIF360's fairness metrics into the model development lifecycle, IBM and its clients were able to identify instances where AI models might produce discriminatory outcomes. This allowed them to take corrective action before deploying these models in critical decision-making processes.

b. Reinforcement of Inequities:

*Impact:*

AI models trained on biased data risk reinforcing existing social inequities. IBM encountered this in sectors such as criminal justice and education, where biased models could exacerbate disparities rather than mitigate them.

*AIF360's Contribution:*

AIF360 helps to prevent this by providing tools that explicitly test

# Dr. Yashwant Aditya

for fairness and equity in model outcomes. By ensuring that AI systems do not disproportionately disadvantage certain groups, IBM aimed to use AIF360 to build models that contribute to social equity.

c. Erosion of Trust:

*Impact:*

Clients and end-users are less likely to trust AI systems that are perceived as biased or unfair. IBM recognized that transparency and fairness are critical for maintaining public trust in AI technologies.

*AIF360's Contribution:*

AIF360 promotes transparency by making it easy for developers to audit models for fairness and share these audits with stakeholders. This openness helps build trust in AI systems by demonstrating a commitment to fairness and accountability.

Despite the multi-faceted nature of bias in complex AI systems complicating the task of addressing these issues, IBM has successfully provided a solution to address these challenges and continues to work on issues even further.

**AIF360's Solutions**

In summary, AIF360, a toolkit developed by IBM, provides a comprehensive set of solutions to address challenges. The toolkit includes:

- Bias Detection:

AIF360 offers various metrics and tests to identify hidden biases in AI models, such as demographic parity tests and error rate analysis.

- Bias Mitigation:

The toolkit provides a range of techniques to mitigate bias, including preprocessing methods, in-processing methods, and post-processing methods.

- Fairness Metrics:

AIF360 offers a comprehensive suite of fairness metrics to evaluate the fairness of AI models, covering aspects like disparate impact, equal opportunity, and predictive parity.

AIF360 is a powerful toolkit for detecting and mitigating bias in AI systems. IBM recognizes the importance of a multi-stakeholder approach to addressing bias in AI. Collaboration across disciplines and engaging with affected communities are essential for developing fair and equitable AI systems.

IBM's development and deployment of the AI Fairness 360 toolkit represent a significant effort to address the challenges of bias in AI systems. By focusing on identifying and correcting these issues, AIF360 has enabled IBM and its clients to develop fairer and more equitable AI solutions. This commitment to responsible AI development helps ensure that AI technologies benefit all users and contribute positively to society.

Dr. Yashwant Aditya

## The Case for Inclusive Innovation

In the rapidly evolving field of Artificial Intelligence (AI), inclusive innovation is not merely a matter of ethical responsibility; it is a strategic advantage that can drive significant advancements and enhance the effectiveness of AI systems. By embracing diversity and striving for equity, the AI community can bring perspectives and insights that contribute to more innovative and impactful technologies. This section explores the benefits of diversity in AI, highlights examples of inclusive innovations, and addresses the challenges and barriers that need to be overcome to achieve true equity in the field.

### Benefits of Diversity in AI

1. Enhanced Creativity and Problem-Solving

One of the most compelling arguments for diversity in AI is the boost it provides to creativity and problem-solving. When individuals from varied backgrounds collaborate, they bring unique perspectives and approaches to the table. This diversity of thought can lead to more innovative solutions and a broader range of ideas.

For example, a diverse AI team may approach a problem from multiple angles, considering factors that a more homogenous group might overlook. This can lead to breakthroughs in AI applications, as the team is more likely to explore unconventional solutions and question assumptions that could limit innovation. Research has

88

shown that diverse teams are more effective at problem-solving and generating creative ideas, which can be particularly valuable in a field as dynamic and complex as AI.

2. Better Representation and Reduced Biases in AI Systems

Diversity within AI teams also helps in creating more representative and fair AI systems. When teams include members from different demographic groups, they are better equipped to identify and address biases in AI models. This leads to the development of systems that more accurately reflect the needs and experiences of a diverse user base.

Biases in AI algorithms often arise from biased training data or assumptions made during the design of the model. For instance, if a facial recognition system is predominantly trained on images of lighter-skinned individuals, it may perform poorly on individuals with darker skin tones. Diverse teams are more likely to recognize such biases and take steps to mitigate them, resulting in AI systems that are more equitable and less likely to reinforce existing inequalities.

**Challenges and Barriers to Achieving Equity**

Despite the benefits of diversity and inclusivity, significant challenges remain in achieving equity in AI. One of the primary issues is the introduction of biases in AI algorithms. Biases can enter

Dr. Yashwant Aditya

AI models through various channels:

- Training Data:

AI systems learn from data, and if the training data is biased or unrepresentative, the AI model will likely produce biased outcomes. For example, if an AI model for job recruitment is trained on historical hiring data that reflects gender biases, it may perpetuate those biases in its recommendations.

- Algorithmic Design:

The design choices made during the development of AI models can also introduce biases. Decisions about which features to include, how to weight them, and how to interpret results can all impact the fairness of the AI system.

The consequences of biased AI systems are significant and can affect various demographic groups differently. For instance, biased AI in criminal justice can lead to unfair treatment or wrongful accusations against marginalized communities. In healthcare, biased diagnostic tools can result in disparities in the quality of care provided to different groups.

**Underrepresentation in AI Fields**

Another major challenge is the underrepresentation of minority groups in AI fields. This underrepresentation manifests in several ways:

- Access to Education and Training:

Many individuals from underrepresented backgrounds face barriers to accessing quality education and training in AI. These barriers include financial constraints, lack of access to advanced educational resources, and limited exposure to STEM fields at an early age.

- Career Advancement:

Even when individuals from diverse backgrounds enter the AI workforce, they often encounter challenges in advancing their careers. These challenges can include bias in hiring and promotion practices, as well as a lack of mentorship and support networks.

To overcome these barriers, it is essential to implement strategies that promote greater inclusivity in AI education and career development. Initiatives such as scholarships for underrepresented students, mentorship programs, and partnerships between industry and educational institutions can help address these challenges and create more equitable opportunities in AI.

The case for inclusive innovation in AI is compelling, as diversity and equity contribute to more creative problem-solving, better representation, and reduced biases in AI systems. Examples of successful inclusive AI innovations highlight the potential of diverse teams to drive meaningful advancements and address pressing social challenges. However, significant challenges remain, including biases in AI algorithms and underrepresentation in the AI workforce. By addressing these challenges and fostering an inclusive environment, the AI community can unlock the full potential of AI technologies and ensure they benefit all segments of society. Embracing diversity and equity in AI is not just a moral imperative but a strategic necessity for shaping a more just and innovative future.

**Strategies for Empowering Diversity and Equity in AI**

To benefit from the full potential of Artificial Intelligence (AI) and ensure it serves all segments of society fairly, it's crucial to implement strategies that promote diversity and equity throughout the field. This involves not only increasing representation within AI teams but also developing systems that are unbiased and inclusive. The following strategies outline effective approaches for achieving these goals:

1. Promoting Inclusive Hiring and Workforce Development

One of the first steps towards a more diverse AI field is to enhance inclusive hiring practices. This includes:

*Diverse Recruitment Channels:*

Expanding recruitment efforts to reach a broader range of candidates can help attract talent from underrepresented groups. This involves partnering with organizations and platforms that focus on diverse talent pools, such as professional networks for women in tech or minority-focused job boards.

*Inclusive Job Descriptions:*

Crafting job descriptions that are welcoming and inclusive can help attract a more diverse applicant pool. Avoiding jargon and emphasizing a commitment to diversity can make positions more appealing to a wider range of candidates.

*Bias-Free Hiring Processes:*

Implementing structured and standardized interview processes can reduce the risk of bias in hiring. Techniques such as blind recruitment, where identifying details are removed from applications, and using diverse hiring panels can help ensure a fairer selection process.

2. Educational Programs and Scholarships Aimed at Underrepresented Groups

Investing in education and training is essential for increasing diversity in the AI field. Key strategies include:

*Scholarships and Financial Support:*

Providing scholarships and financial assistance for students from underrepresented backgrounds can help alleviate the financial barriers that often limit access to AI education. Programs like the

AI4ALL Foundation offer scholarships and summer programs to underrepresented high school students interested in AI.

*Mentorship and Support Networks:*

Establishing mentorship programs that connect experienced AI professionals with newcomers from diverse backgrounds can provide valuable guidance and support. These networks help mentees navigate career challenges and build connections within the industry.

*STEM Outreach Programs:*

Engaging with younger students through outreach programs and STEM education initiatives can inspire interest in AI and technology from an early age. Programs that introduce diverse students to AI concepts and careers can help build a pipeline of future talent.

3. Techniques for Identifying and Mitigating Biases in AI Algorithms

Developing AI systems that are fair and unbiased requires a proactive approach to identifying and mitigating biases. Key techniques include:

*Diverse Data Collection:*

Ensuring that training data is representative of diverse populations is crucial for creating unbiased AI systems. This involves collecting data from various sources and demographic groups to avoid skewed results.

*Bias Detection Tools*:

Utilizing tools and frameworks designed to detect biases in AI models can help identify potential issues early in the development process. Techniques such as fairness audits and impact assessments can evaluate how an AI system performs across different demographic groups.

*Algorithmic Transparency*:

Promoting transparency in AI algorithms allows for better scrutiny and understanding of how decisions are made. Explaining AI model outputs and involving external audits can help ensure that systems are fair and accountable.

Plausible Predictions for the Impact of Inclusive AI on Various Industries

The vision for a diverse AI future encompasses several key goals and aspirations:

- Universal Accessibility and Fairness:

One of the primary goals is to ensure that AI technologies are accessible and fair to all individuals, regardless of their background. This includes designing AI systems that address the needs of underrepresented and marginalized groups, ensuring that technologies do not perpetuate existing biases or inequalities.

- Diverse Talent Pools:

Achieving long-term equity in AI involves building diverse talent pools by improving access to AI education and careers for underrepresented groups. This includes creating educational pathways, mentorship opportunities, and supportive networks to foster a more inclusive workforce.

- Inclusive Innovation:

Another aspiration is to drive innovation through diverse perspectives. By incorporating a wide range of viewpoints and experiences, AI development can lead to more creative and effective solutions that address global challenges and improve quality of life.

- Ethical and Transparent AI:

Ensuring that AI systems are developed and deployed with ethical considerations at the forefront is crucial. This includes transparency in AI decision-making processes, accountability for outcomes, and ongoing efforts to address biases and inequities.

**To create a more inclusive and equitable future in artificial intelligence, we must actively promote diversity in the AI workforce, address bias in AI systems, adhere to ethical principles in AI development, invest in education and training**

programs to foster AI skills, and foster collaboration among stakeholders. By working together, we can ensure that AI benefits society as a whole and avoids unintended negative consequences.

# Multiple-Choice Questions

1. **Why is diversity important in AI development?**
   a) It helps AI systems generate faster responses.
   b) It ensures that AI systems reflect the experiences and needs of a broader range of users.
   c) It prevents bias and reduces the risk of AI reinforcing stereotypes.
   d) It makes AI development more expensive.

2. **What is the primary goal of equity in AI?**
   a) To ensure everyone has equal opportunities and resources in AI development and usage.
   b) To make AI development faster and cheaper.
   c) To prioritize certain groups over others in AI training datasets.
   d) To remove all human oversight from AI decision-making.

3. **Which of the following is an example of inclusive innovation in AI?**
   a) Developing AI-driven medical diagnostic tools trained on data from diverse populations.
   b) Creating AI-powered hiring systems that only consider candidates from a specific demographic.
   c) Designing AI voice assistants that recognize multiple accents and languages.
   d) Training AI solely on data from Western countries.

4. **What risks arise from a lack of diversity in AI development teams?**
a) AI models may perpetuate existing biases and inequalities.
b) AI systems might not perform accurately for all demographic groups.
c) Companies might lose potential markets by developing non-inclusive AI products.
d) AI will become more expensive to implement.

5. **How can businesses benefit from prioritizing diversity and equity in AI?**
a) They can tap into new customer segments and expand their market reach.
b) They can build greater trust with users who see their needs reflected in AI solutions.
c) They can eliminate the need for AI regulation.
d) They can improve the accuracy and fairness of their AI systems.

6. **Which of the following factors contribute to diversity in AI?** *(Select all that apply.)*
☐ Ethnicity and race
☐ Gender representation
☐ Socioeconomic status
☐ Cultural background
☐ Disability inclusion

7. **Why is diverse training data important for AI models?**
a) It helps AI systems make more informed and fair decisions.
b) It eliminates all potential biases in AI systems.
c) It allows AI models to be effective across different populations.
d) It reduces the need for human oversight in AI decision-making.

8. **What is a potential negative consequence of AI systems that are not trained on diverse data?**

a) AI models may produce biased or unfair outcomes.
b) AI systems may not recognize or properly serve underrepresented groups.
c) AI will be completely useless for all applications.
d) AI will work better but only for a limited audience.

9. **Which of the following are ways to promote equity in AI?** *(Select all that apply.)*

☐ Ensuring diverse representation in AI development teams.

☐ Regularly auditing AI systems for bias.

☐ Providing fair access to AI education and career opportunities.

☐ Limiting AI training to only one demographic group.

10. **What is one of the most significant benefits of inclusive innovation in AI?**

a) It ensures AI technologies are more effective and widely accepted.
b) It increases profits for technology companies only.
c) It eliminates the need for human involvement in AI governance.
d) It makes AI systems more complex and difficult to understand.

# Answers Key:

**1. Why is diversity important in AI development?**

**b)** It ensures that AI systems reflect the experiences and needs of a broader range of users.

**c)** It prevents bias and reduces the risk of AI reinforcing stereotypes.

Dr. Yashwant Aditya

**2. What is the primary goal of equity in AI?**

**a)** To ensure everyone has equal opportunities and resources in AI development and usage.

**3. Which of the following is an example of inclusive innovation in AI?**

**a)** Developing AI-driven medical diagnostic tools trained on data from diverse populations.

**c)** Designing AI voice assistants that recognize multiple accents and languages.

**4. What risks arise from a lack of diversity in AI development teams?**

**a)** AI models may perpetuate existing biases and inequalities.

**b)** AI systems might not perform accurately for all demographic groups.

**c)** Companies might lose potential markets by developing non-inclusive AI products.

**5. How can businesses benefit from prioritizing diversity and equity in AI?**

**a)** They can tap into new customer segments and expand their market reach.

**b)** They can build greater trust with users who see their needs reflected in AI solutions.

**d)** They can improve the accuracy and fairness of their AI systems.

**6. Which of the following factors contribute to diversity in AI? (Select all that apply.)**

☑ Ethnicity and race

☑ Gender representation

☑ Socioeconomic status

☑ Cultural background

☑ Disability inclusion

**7. Why is diverse training data important for AI models?**

**a)** It helps AI systems make more informed and fair decisions.

**c)** It allows AI models to be effective across different populations.

**8. What is a potential negative consequence of AI systems that are not trained on diverse data?**

**a)** AI models may produce biased or unfair outcomes.

**b)** AI systems may not recognize or properly serve underrepresented groups.

**9. Which of the following are ways to promote equity in AI? (Select all that apply.)**

☑ Ensuring diverse representation in AI development teams

☑ Regularly auditing AI systems for bias

☑ Providing fair access to AI education and career opportunities

**10. What is one of the most significant benefits of inclusive**

**innovation in AI?**

**a)** It ensures AI technologies are more effective and widely accepted.

# Chapter 6:
# Building an AI-Ready Culture

The world is buzzing with AI—everybody wants a piece of it, from small startups to large corporations. But here's the thing: jumping into AI without understanding if your business is ready is like diving into deep water without knowing how to swim. Before embarking on the AI journey, it's essential to assess whether you're truly prepared for this leap. Let's break it down, step by step, so you can honestly evaluate if your organization is AI-ready.

### Understanding the Basics

The first question to ask yourself is: Do you understand AI well enough to implement it? AI is more than just a buzzword. It's a collection of technologies that includes machine learning, natural language processing, and computer vision, among others. The common misconception is that AI is a magic solution that will solve all problems, but the reality is more complex. If you're not familiar with the fundamentals, start by educating yourself and your team.

That doesn't mean you need to be an AI expert, but you should understand how AI works, the data it relies on, and what problems it can (or cannot) solve. If AI feels like a foreign language to your leadership team, this might be a signal that you're not quite ready—

yet.

## Data: The Lifeblood of AI

AI runs on data—lots and lots of data. Ask yourself, Do we have access to quality data? If your organization doesn't have clean, organized, and accessible data, implementing AI will be like trying to drive a car without fuel. AI algorithms learn and make decisions based on the data you feed them, so if that data is incomplete or inaccurate, AI won't be able to perform well.

Data is more than just numbers and spreadsheets. It's about the quality and relevance of that data to your specific business challenges. Are you capturing the right data from your customers, operations, and market? And even more importantly, is your data structured and ready to be processed by AI systems? For many organizations, this is the first major hurdle.

## Talent and Skills

Now, let's talk about people. Do you have the right talent in place? AI doesn't just run itself—at least not yet. You need a team of people who understand AI, can work with the data, and know how to integrate AI solutions into your business operations. If you lack this talent, don't worry—it's a common challenge. However, it's something you'll need to address before moving forward.

You may need data scientists, AI engineers, or machine learning specialists, but beyond that, you'll need people who understand the business side of things, too. They'll need to translate AI capabilities into actual business value. A diverse, multi-skilled team is essential for ensuring your AI project's success.

## Culture and Mindset

An AI-ready culture isn't just about having the right technology or people. Is your company's mindset ready for AI? AI is disruptive, and it's going to change how your organization works. This means being open to change and innovation, even when it feels uncomfortable. If your company is stuck in traditional ways of thinking, AI adoption might be a rough road. Embrace curiosity, experimentation, and adaptability.

AI adoption isn't a "set it and forget it" kind of initiative. It's an ongoing process of learning, adjusting, and improving. Your organization needs to foster a culture that is comfortable with these ongoing cycles of iteration.

## Investment and Commitment

Finally, ask yourself, Are you committed to investing in AI for the long haul? AI is not a short-term fix. It requires significant investment—not just in technology but in people, processes, and change management. If you're looking for a quick win, AI might not be the best option. AI implementations can take months, sometimes even years, to show real, impactful results.

That said, if you're ready to commit the necessary time, resources, and energy, AI can revolutionize the way your business operates and competes.

**Take the AI-Readiness Quiz**

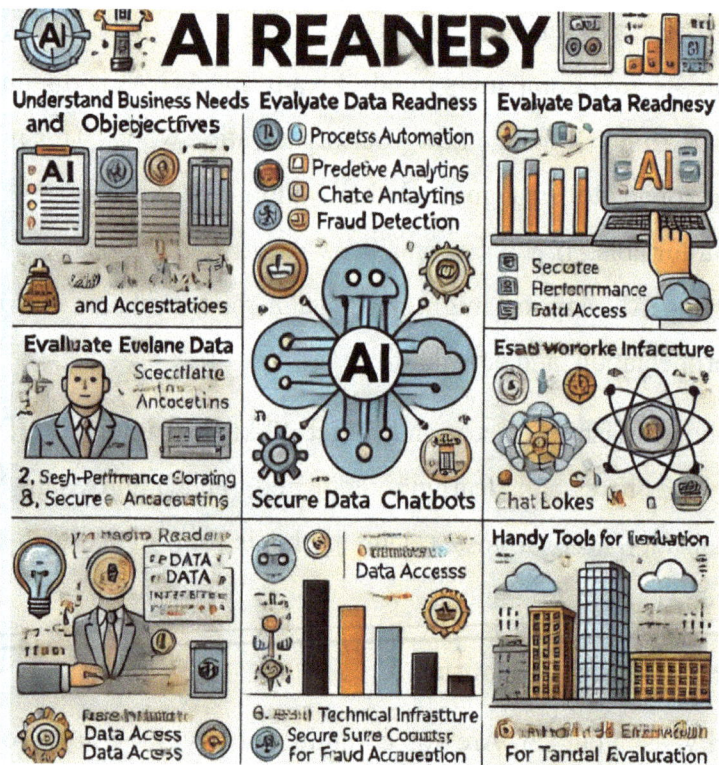

*Figure 1 Everything AI*

To truly evaluate your readiness for AI, it might be helpful to conduct an internal AI-readiness quiz. Ask key stakeholders to answer questions like:

- *Do we have access to the data we need?*
- *Is our leadership team knowledgeable about AI technologies?*
- *Are our employees ready for a shift in how they work?*
- *Do we have the right talent in-house, or do we need to invest in hiring?*
- *Are we financially and organizationally prepared to invest in AI over the long term?*

This self-assessment can help you see where you stand and what gaps you may need to fill before diving into AI.

**Building the Case for AI**

Now that you've assessed whether your organization is AI-ready, it's time to build a strong case for adopting AI. It's not just about technology—convincing stakeholders to embrace AI requires solid reasoning, evidence of benefits, and a clear understanding of how it aligns with your business goals. Let's dive into how you can construct a convincing argument that resonates with decision-makers.

**Start with the Why: What Problems Can AI Solve?**

The foundation of any AI implementation is knowing why you need it. What specific problem are you trying to solve with AI? Is it improving customer service, optimizing operations, enhancing decision-making, or gaining a competitive edge? Identifying the problem is crucial because it gives you a clear direction and sets the tone for your AI strategy.

For example, let's say your business struggles with managing customer queries due to high call volumes. Instead of hiring more customer service agents, which can be costly and inefficient, AI-powered chatbots can automate responses to common questions, providing 24/7 support and freeing up human agents to handle more complex issues. In this case, AI solves a specific pain point while improving efficiency and customer satisfaction.

By clearly identifying the problems AI can address, you give your stakeholders a concrete reason to consider the technology. Keep the focus on solving business problems rather than chasing AI for its own sake.

**Show the ROI: How Will AI Benefit Your Business?**

Once you've identified the problem, the next step is to demonstrate the return on investment (ROI) AI can deliver. This can be tricky because AI benefits aren't always immediate or easily measurable, but they are real. Start by showing how AI can increase efficiency, reduce costs, or drive revenue.

For instance, AI can automate time-consuming tasks like data entry, which reduces human error and allows employees to focus on more strategic activities. AI-powered analytics can help you make smarter decisions faster, giving you insights into customer behavior, market trends, or operational inefficiencies that were previously hidden.

Consider this example: A retail company adopts AI to optimize its inventory management. Instead of relying on guesswork, AI analyzes sales patterns, seasonal trends, and other variables to predict the optimal stock levels. As a result, the company reduces overstock, avoids stockouts, and ultimately boosts profits. This is a tangible, measurable outcome of AI's impact on the bottom line.

Be sure to tailor your ROI analysis to your specific business context. Use examples relevant to your industry and, if possible, gather data from case studies that show how similar companies have benefited from AI.

**Address Fears and Concerns:**

**AI Isn't Here to Replace Everyone**

One of the biggest barriers to AI adoption is fear. Employees and even leaders often worry that AI will replace jobs, create an impersonal work environment, or introduce too much complexity. Addressing these concerns head-on is a key part of building your case for AI.

Start by acknowledging that AI does automate tasks, but that doesn't necessarily mean it will replace people. Instead, AI can augment human capabilities by taking over repetitive, mundane tasks and allowing employees to focus on higher-value work. For instance, AI might handle data analysis while humans interpret those insights to make strategic decisions.

Take the healthcare industry as an example. AI-powered diagnostic tools can analyze medical images faster and more accurately than humans, but doctors still need to make the final call and provide compassionate care to patients. In this case, AI enhances the doctors' capabilities rather than replacing them.

Make it clear that AI is a tool—one that empowers employees to be more efficient, creative, and impactful. Addressing concerns around job security, training, and ethical implications will help foster a positive view of AI.

**Build a Vision:**

**What Does AI-Driven Success Look Like?**

Once you've addressed the practical aspects, paint a picture of what success with AI looks like. Help your stakeholders visualize how AI can transform the organization. This could mean streamlining operations, making faster decisions, personalizing customer experiences, or unlocking new revenue streams.

For instance, imagine a marketing team leveraging AI to create hyper-personalized campaigns. Instead of guessing what customers want, AI analyzes individual preferences and behaviors to deliver tailored messages at the right time. This not only improves customer satisfaction but also increases conversion rates and revenue. Stakeholders can more easily get on board when they see a clear, compelling vision of what's possible with AI.

Share success stories from other companies, especially those in similar industries. For example, Amazon's use of AI in logistics and recommendation systems has transformed the way they do business, resulting in increased sales and customer loyalty. Such examples can inspire your team and show that AI-driven success is achievable.

**Emphasize Scalability and Future-Proofing**

Another strong argument for AI adoption is its scalability and future-proofing potential. AI isn't just a short-term fix—it's an investment in the future. The beauty of AI is that it can scale with your business. As your organization grows, AI systems can adapt to new challenges, new data, and new goals.

Let's take the example of a logistics company. Initially, AI might be implemented to optimize delivery routes. As the business expands, the AI system can be scaled up to handle more complex operations, like warehouse automation or predictive maintenance for delivery trucks. AI's ability to grow with your business ensures that you're not just solving today's problems but preparing for tomorrow's opportunities.

Dr. Yashwant Aditya

Additionally, adopting AI positions your organization as a forward-thinking, innovative leader in your industry. As AI becomes more embedded in everyday business, organizations that fail to adopt it may fall behind. Show your stakeholders that AI isn't just about solving problems—it's about staying competitive and resilient in a rapidly changing world.

**The Power of Collaboration:**

**Why You Need a Multi-Disciplinary AI SWAT Team**

AI may be at the cutting edge of technology, but that doesn't mean it belongs exclusively in the hands of your IT department or data scientists. To truly harness the power of AI, you need a multi-disciplinary team—a diverse group of people who bring unique skills and perspectives to the table. This AI SWAT team will be the driving force behind successfully integrating AI into your organization. Here's why collaboration is the secret ingredient.

**Why Multi-Disciplinary Matters**

AI isn't just a technical tool—it's a transformational force that impacts nearly every aspect of your business. From customer service to finance to marketing, AI can touch multiple departments. That's why a multi-disciplinary approach is crucial. You need people who understand the technology, but you also need those who know how to apply it to specific business problems.

Imagine trying to implement an AI-driven customer support chatbot without the input of your customer service team. Sure, the chatbot might work from a technical standpoint, but it could fall flat if it doesn't meet the actual needs of your customers. Likewise, your marketing department might have insights that are critical to building personalized AI-powered campaigns. Each team has a piece of the puzzle, and only by working together can you create a complete picture.

The power of this diversity lies in cross-functional collaboration. Each person brings a different perspective, which helps ensure that AI solutions are practical, effective, and aligned with overall business goals.

**The Anatomy of a Multi-Disciplinary AI Team**

Let's break down what a strong AI SWAT team might look like. While the specific roles will vary depending on your organization, here are some key players to consider:

*Data Scientists and AI Engineers*: These are your technical experts—the ones who build the models, write the algorithms and manage the data. They are essential for the technical development of AI solutions.

*Business Analysts*: These folks bridge the gap between technology and business. They help identify opportunities where AI can provide value and work with the technical team to ensure AI solutions align with business goals.

*Domain Experts*: These are the people who understand your business inside and out. Whether they're from marketing, finance, customer service, or operations, their insights are crucial for developing AI solutions that solve real-world problems.

*Project Managers*: AI projects can be complex, so you'll need someone who can coordinate efforts, manage timelines, and ensure that the project stays on track.

*Ethics and Compliance Officers*: AI raises unique ethical challenges, such as data privacy concerns, algorithmic bias, and transparency issues. Having someone who can navigate these complexities is crucial to ensuring your AI efforts remain ethical and compliant with regulations.

*Executives and Decision-Makers*: Ultimately, AI adoption requires buy-in from the top. Executives help set the vision and make the big-picture decisions that will guide the AI initiative.

This team may vary in size and composition depending on the scope of your AI project, but the key is to ensure representation from a wide array of disciplines.

**Fostering Collaboration Within the Team**

Once you've assembled your multi-disciplinary team, the next challenge is fostering collaboration. This is easier said than done—different departments often have different ways of thinking, working, and communicating. But successful AI adoption requires breaking down silos and encouraging open communication and collaboration across departments.

Here are some strategies to foster collaboration within your AI SWAT team:

*Create a Common Language*: The tech team may talk in algorithms and data models, while the business side speaks in customer metrics and revenue goals. Encourage the team to create a common language so everyone understands the core concepts of AI and how they translate to business value.

*Set Clear Goals*: Make sure everyone is on the same page about what you're trying to achieve with AI. This will help the team stay focused and aligned, even as they tackle complex challenges from different angles.

*Encourage Open Dialogue*: Create an environment where team members feel comfortable sharing their perspectives, even if they come from different disciplines. Sometimes, the best ideas come from the most unexpected places.

*Promote Continuous Learning*: AI is an evolving field, and new developments are happening all the time. Encourage your team to keep learning, whether through training, workshops, or simply sharing knowledge with one another.

*Celebrate Small Wins*: AI implementation can be a long, winding road, so take time to celebrate milestones along the way. This helps keep the team motivated and reminds everyone that their efforts are paying off.

**Success Stories of AI SWAT Teams in Action**

Now, let's take a look at some real-world success stories where multi-disciplinary teams were critical to AI implementation.

One well-known example comes from the retail giant Walmart. Walmart's AI team isn't just made up of tech experts—they include people from merchandising, logistics, and even store management. This multi-disciplinary approach helped them develop an AI system to optimize inventory management, ensuring that shelves are always stocked with the right products at the right time. By combining insights from different areas of the business, Walmart was able to create a solution that significantly improved efficiency and customer satisfaction.

Another example is Spotify, which leverages AI to create personalized playlists for its users. Spotify's AI team includes engineers, data scientists, music experts, and marketers. This diversity allows them to build AI systems that understand both the technical side of music recommendation algorithms and the human element of music preferences. As a result, Spotify's AI-driven playlists are beloved by users and have helped the company grow its subscriber base.

These examples show how multi-disciplinary AI teams can drive innovation and success. When people from different backgrounds and areas of expertise come together, they can build AI solutions that are more effective, impactful, and aligned with business needs.

**The Bottom Line: Collaboration is Key to AI Success**

In the end, AI isn't just about technology—it's about people. No single department can implement AI in isolation. By bringing together a multidisciplinary team, you ensure that your AI initiatives are grounded in real business needs, are technically sound, and have the buy-in necessary to succeed.

Collaboration is the lifeblood of AI implementation. With the right people working together, you can unlock the true potential of AI for your organization.

Now that you've built a multi-disciplinary AI team, it's time to take one of the most critical steps in your AI journey: securing organization-wide buy-in. While having a strong AI team is essential, getting everyone across the organization on board is equally important. AI implementation isn't just about technology—it's about culture, mindset, and changing the way your organization thinks and operates. Without buy-in from all levels of the business, even the best AI strategies can fall flat. Let's explore how you can successfully get your organization on board.

## Why Organization-Wide Buy-In Matters

One of the biggest mistakes companies make when adopting AI is assuming that it's something only the IT or data team needs to worry about. AI impacts the entire organization, and its success depends on widespread adoption and acceptance. Without buy-in, AI initiatives can face resistance, lack of engagement, or, worst of all, outright failure.

For example, if the marketing team doesn't see the value in AI-driven analytics, they might continue making decisions based on gut instincts rather than data. Similarly, if customer service agents feel threatened by AI chatbots, they might resist integrating AI into their workflow, leading to inefficiencies and frustration.

Getting buy-in means helping everyone in the organization understand how AI can enhance their work, solve their problems, and ultimately contribute to the company's success. When people feel like they're part of the process, they're more likely to support AI initiatives rather than push back against them.

## Start from the Top: Executive Buy-In

The first step in securing organization-wide buy-in is getting support from the leadership team. Executives set the tone for the rest of the organization, and their commitment to AI adoption will significantly influence how it's received throughout the company. AI initiatives can lack the resources, attention, and strategic alignment they need to succeed without executive buy-in.

To get executives on board, you'll need to speak their language. Focus on the strategic benefits of AI—how it can drive growth, improve efficiency, and give the company a competitive edge. Use data and case studies to show how AI has transformed other companies in your industry, and be clear about the ROI they can expect. Executives are more likely to back AI initiatives if they see them as key drivers of the company's future success.

Additionally, address any concerns they may have. Executives might worry about the cost of AI implementation, the risk of failure, or the potential impact on the workforce. Be prepared to discuss these issues openly and provide reassurance. For example, show how AI can be implemented in phases to manage costs and risks and emphasize that AI is a tool to augment human capabilities, not replace them.

**Middle Management:**

**The Key to Implementation**

Once you have executive support, the next step is getting middle

Dr. Yashwant Aditya

management on board. Middle managers play a crucial role in AI adoption because they're the ones who will oversee the implementation process within their teams. If they're not convinced of AI's value or feel uncertain about how to use it, they could unintentionally hinder its success.

To gain middle management buy-in, emphasize how AI can make their jobs easier and improve their team's performance. For instance, AI-powered analytics can give managers deeper insights into their team's productivity, allowing them to make more informed decisions. AI tools can automate administrative tasks, freeing up managers to focus on leadership and strategy.

It's also essential to provide managers with the training and support they need to feel confident using AI tools. Offer workshops, webinars, or hands-on training sessions that show how AI can be integrated into their existing workflows. Managers who feel empowered and capable will be more likely to champion AI within their teams.

**Educating Employees: From Fear to Enthusiasm**

At the grassroots level, employees are often the ones who will interact with AI daily, so getting their buy-in is critical. However, employees may have concerns about AI—such as fear of job loss, apprehension about new technology, or skepticism about its benefits. Education and communication are key to addressing these

120

concerns and turning fear into enthusiasm.

Start by being transparent about what AI will and won't do. Make it clear that AI isn't here to replace jobs but to assist employees by taking over repetitive tasks, providing insights, and enabling them to focus on more meaningful work. For example, in customer service, AI can handle simple inquiries, allowing human agents to focus on complex, high-touch interactions.

It's also important to highlight success stories within the organization. If a particular department has implemented AI and seen positive results, share that story with the rest of the company. Success breeds success, and employees are more likely to get excited about AI when they see real-life examples of how it's making their colleagues' work easier and more effective.

Lastly, employees should ensure they have the training and resources to work with AI. This could include online tutorials, in-person workshops, or a dedicated support team to answer questions and troubleshoot issues. When employees feel confident in using AI tools, they'll be more open to embracing the technology.

**Building a Culture of AI Adoption**

AI isn't a one-and-done initiative—it's an ongoing journey that requires a culture of adoption. Building this culture means embedding AI into the fabric of your organization, making it a natural part of how you work and think.

One way to foster this culture is by celebrating AI successes. When an AI initiative delivers positive results—improved efficiency, cost savings, or enhanced customer satisfaction—make sure to recognize and celebrate those wins. This could be through internal newsletters, company-wide announcements, or even awards and incentives for teams implementing AI successfully. Celebrating successes reinforces the message that AI is valuable and worth investing in.

Another key to building a culture of AI adoption is encouraging continuous learning. AI is an evolving field, and there will always be new developments, tools, and best practices to explore. Encourage employees at all levels to keep learning about AI and experimenting with new ways to use it. This could include offering access to AI-related courses, hosting internal AI hackathons, or creating cross-departmental AI working groups.

Finally, keep the conversation about AI going. Hold regular meetings or forums where employees can share their experiences with AI, discuss challenges, and brainstorm new ideas. Keeping AI at the forefront of your mind helps ensure that it becomes an integral part of your organization's strategy and operations.

**Measuring and Communicating AI's Impact**

As you implement AI across the organization, it's crucial to measure its impact and communicate those results clearly. Tracking the success of your AI initiatives helps you refine and improve your approach and provides valuable evidence to support continued investment in AI.

Start by defining key performance indicators (KPIs) that align with your business goals. These might include metrics like cost savings, efficiency improvements, increased revenue, customer satisfaction, or employee productivity. Regularly track and analyze these metrics to assess the performance of your AI initiatives.

Once you have the data, communicate the results to the rest of the organization. Share updates on how AI is driving positive outcomes and helping the company achieve its objectives. Transparency is key—when people see the tangible benefits of AI, they're more likely to support it.

Use this data to continue building momentum for AI adoption. If an AI project shows strong results, use it as a case study to make the case for expanding AI initiatives in other areas of the business.

**Measuring and Communicating AI's Impact**

Measuring and communicating the impact of AI is not just a nice-to-have—it's a critical step in ensuring the long-term success of your AI initiatives. Success breeds success, and clear, data-backed communication helps maintain momentum, ensuring that AI becomes ingrained in your organization's DNA.

Dr. Yashwant Aditya

## Start with the Right Metrics

To truly understand the impact of your AI initiatives, it's essential to choose the right key performance indicators (KPIs) that align with your organization's goals. While traditional business metrics like revenue growth, cost reduction, and productivity improvements are essential, AI also presents unique opportunities to track more nuanced outcomes.

## Consider the following KPIs:

*Operational Efficiency*: Track how AI-driven automation has streamlined workflows, reduced manual labor, or sped up decision-making processes. For example, time savings can be measured from AI-enhanced customer support or AI-powered supply chain optimization.

*Customer Satisfaction*: Gauge the impact AI has had on customer interactions. Has AI-driven personalization increased customer loyalty? Have AI-powered chatbots improved response times and satisfaction scores?

*Cost Savings*: AI implementations often promise cost reductions. Are you saving money by automating routine tasks? Is AI helping you reduce operational costs in ways that weren't previously possible?

*Innovation & Growth*: Track how AI is enabling innovation. Are new AI-driven products or services being developed? Is AI helping you gain new market share or open new revenue streams?

These metrics should be periodically reviewed and refined as your AI initiatives evolve. As you become more experienced with AI, you may discover new metrics that better reflect the value AI is delivering to your organization.

**Communicating Results: The Power of Storytelling**

Once you've collected the data, you must communicate your results effectively to your organization. But remember, people don't connect with numbers—they connect with stories. Use data to tell a compelling story about how AI is transforming your company.

For example, instead of just reporting that AI saved X dollars, frame the data within a success story. Perhaps AI helped your customer support team reduce response times by 40%, leading to higher customer satisfaction and retention. Or maybe AI automation freed up your sales team to focus on building stronger relationships with key clients, resulting in new deals.

Here's how to approach communication for different audiences:

*Executive Leadership*: Focus on how AI is helping the company meet its strategic objectives. Show them the big-picture outcomes, like increased revenue, improved competitiveness, or enhanced operational efficiency. Highlight the ROI and discuss how AI fits into the company's long-term vision.

*Middle Management*: Emphasize how AI is making their teams more effective and efficient. Show managers how AI is helping them hit their targets and enhance their team's performance. Use success stories from other departments as examples they can apply within their own teams.

*Employees*: Share how AI is improving their day-to-day work. Highlight specific tools and processes that AI has improved and show how these changes are making their jobs easier, more enjoyable, or more impactful. Make it clear that AI is empowering them rather than replacing them.

By framing AI successes as tangible, relatable improvements, you can build excitement and enthusiasm around AI initiatives at all levels of the organization. When people see the positive results of AI in action, they'll be more inclined to support and engage with future AI projects.

**Feedback Loops and Continuous Improvement**

AI adoption is not a linear process—it's a cycle of continuous improvement. Even as you begin to see positive results from AI, it's essential to remain open to feedback and refinement. AI systems can become even more effective with time, but only if you constantly evaluate their performance and make adjustments as needed.

Establish feedback loops throughout your AI initiatives. Collect feedback from different stakeholders, including executives, managers, employees, and customers. This feedback can help you identify areas where AI is excelling and where there's room for improvement.

**For instance:**

*Employees*: Are they finding AI tools helpful or struggling with implementation? Are there any unintended consequences of AI adoption that need to be addressed, such as increased workloads due to over-reliance on AI?

*Managers*: Are AI-driven insights leading to better decision-making? Are there any bottlenecks in how AI is being deployed within teams? Could AI tools be customized further to fit the unique needs of each department?

*Customers*: How are customers responding to AI-enhanced products or services? Are there any aspects of AI-driven customer interactions that could be improved to enhance satisfaction or loyalty?

Use this feedback to continuously refine and optimize your AI systems. Remember, AI is a dynamic field, and staying agile is essential for keeping up with advances in technology and changing market conditions.

Dr. Yashwant Aditya

**Scaling AI Across the Organization**

Once you've successfully implemented AI in specific areas of the business, the next step is to scale it across the organization. Scaling AI requires a thoughtful approach, which involves expanding AI initiatives while ensuring consistency, quality, and continued buy-in.

Here are some strategies for scaling AI effectively:

*Standardization*: Develop standardized frameworks for AI implementation that can be replicated across different departments. This might include best practices for data management, tool selection, and integration processes.

*Cross-Departmental Collaboration*: Encourage collaboration between departments to share AI insights, tools, and success stories. For example, if the marketing team has successfully implemented AI-driven personalization, other departments could adopt similar techniques to improve their processes.

*AI Champions*: Identify and empower AI champions across different departments. These individuals can act as liaisons between their teams and the central AI strategy, helping to ensure smooth implementation and fostering a culture of innovation.

*Phased Expansion*: Roll out AI initiatives in phases to ensure scalability without overwhelming teams. Start with smaller-scale projects in new departments, then gradually expand to larger initiatives as AI adoption matures.

As AI becomes more integrated into your organization, it's also important to maintain a clear vision for the future. Regularly revisit your AI strategy to ensure it aligns with your company's evolving goals and priorities. Scaling AI should always be driven by the broader business objectives, not just the pursuit of technology for its own sake.

**The Role of Leadership in Sustaining AI Adoption**

Finally, leadership plays a critical role in sustaining AI adoption over the long term. While AI might start as a project driven by specific teams or departments, it must eventually become part of the company's overall culture and strategic vision. This requires consistent leadership support and guidance.

Leaders should continue championing AI initiatives, providing the necessary resources, attention, and focus to ensure their success. AI adoption isn't just about implementing technology—it's about transforming how your organization operates. This transformation needs to be nurtured by leadership at every level.

Moreover, leaders must foster an environment of curiosity and innovation. Encourage teams to experiment with AI, explore new use cases, and push the possible boundaries. When people are empowered to innovate, AI can become a powerful tool for driving growth, competitiveness, and long-term success.

# Is Your Organization Ready for AI?

## Section 1: Understanding the Basics of AI

**1.1 Do you understand the core concepts of AI, such as machine learning, natural language processing, and computer vision?**

- ⌐ Yes, I have a solid understanding.
- ⌐ I know the basics but could learn more.
- ⌐ No, I have limited or no knowledge.

**1.2 Has your leadership team been educated about AI and its potential applications?**

- ⌐ Yes, they are well-informed.
- ⌐ They are aware but need more information.
- ⌐ No, they haven't explored AI in detail.

*Reflection:*
Do you need to invest in educating yourself and your leadership team about AI? List any specific areas where you need more knowledge.

## Section 2: Data – The Lifeblood of AI

**2.1 Do you have access to high-quality data that is relevant to your business needs?**

- ⌐ Yes, we have well-organized and relevant data.
- ⌐ We have data, but it's incomplete or inconsistent.
- ⌐ No, we struggle to capture and organize useful data.

**2.2 Is your data structured and easily accessible for AI systems to process?**

- ⌐ Yes, our data is structured for AI use.
- ⌐ Our data is somewhat organized but needs improvements.
- ⌐ No, our data is not ready for AI integration.

*Reflection:*
What steps can you take to ensure your data is ready for AI? Do you need to invest in data infrastructure or data cleaning?

## Section 3: Talent and Skills

**3.1 Does your team have the necessary expertise to implement AI (e.g., data scientists, AI engineers, business analysts)?**

- ⌐ Yes, we have the right talent.
- ⌐ We have some skills, but we need more specialized expertise.
- ⌐ No, we lack the talent required for AI implementation.

**3.2 Do your employees understand the potential impact of AI on their roles and are they open to change?**

- ⌐ Yes, they are prepared and eager for change.

- ⌐ Some employees are ready, but others may need support.
- ⌐ No, there is resistance to AI adoption.

*Reflection:*
Consider if you need to hire new talent or train existing employees to build a diverse, multi-skilled team. How will you address resistance to change?

## Section 4: Culture and Mindset

### 4.1 Is your company's culture open to experimentation and continuous learning?

- ⌐ Yes, we foster innovation and adaptability.
- ⌐ We are open to change but struggle with consistent innovation.
- ⌐ No, our company is resistant to change.

### 4.2 Does your company embrace the concept of iterative improvement and adjustment?

- ⌐ Yes, we view changes as opportunities for growth.
- ⌐ We are somewhat open, but it's not ingrained in our culture.
- ⌐ No, we prefer to stick to traditional methods.

*Reflection:*
How can you build a mindset that embraces AI and innovation? What cultural changes would help AI adoption succeed in your organization?

## Section 5: Investment and Commitment

**5.1 Are you willing to commit time, resources, and financial investment to AI in the long term?**

- ⌐ Yes, we are prepared for long-term commitment.
- ⌐ We are open but cautious about long-term investments.
- ⌐ No, we are only interested in short-term results.

**5.2 Have you considered the change management efforts necessary to implement AI successfully?**

- ⌐ Yes, we have a plan in place for managing change.
- ⌐ We are aware but haven't developed a clear plan.
- ⌐ No, we haven't thought about change management.

*Reflection:*
What resources will you need to allocate for AI implementation, and how will you manage the organizational changes that come with it?

# Chapter 7:
# AI and Leadership

## Unlocking New Possibilities in Governance and Strategy

In the ever-evolving business landscape, one thing has become crystal clear: AI is not just a tool for automation or data processing anymore. It has become a significant player in leadership and governance. The ways we make decisions, collaborate, and strategize are transforming thanks to AI's growing influence. As a leader, understanding AI's potential is no longer optional—it's crucial.

## Ethics and Governance

First things first: AI comes with a lot of power, but as the saying goes, with great power comes great responsibility. Leaders must understand the ethical implications of integrating AI into their decision-making processes.

## The Double-Edged Sword of AI Ethics

AI is often hailed for its ability to process vast amounts of data and deliver insights faster than any human could. AI offers a competitive edge, from predicting customer behavior to optimizing supply chains. However, there's a catch: AI systems are only as good as the data they're fed. AI can perpetuate inequalities and make poor decisions if that data is biased or incomplete.

Take hiring algorithms, for example. Several high-profile companies have attempted to use AI to streamline the hiring process. Yet, without careful oversight, these systems can unintentionally favor one demographic over another, leading to discrimination. AI doesn't have its ethics—it inherits the biases of the people who create and train it. That's why governance is essential. Leaders must ensure their AI systems are aligned with ethical standards, ensuring fairness, transparency, and accountability.

**Establishing AI Governance Frameworks**

Governance is the glue that holds ethics and AI together. This means creating frameworks that guide how AI is used within an organization. These frameworks should include guidelines for data management, decision-making, and accountability. For example, leaders need to ensure that AI systems are transparent—meaning the decision-making process can be explained and understood by humans. If an AI model suggests a strategic change, decision-makers should be able to trace back the data and logic behind that recommendation.

A good governance framework also addresses data privacy. As AI systems process massive amounts of personal and sensitive information, leaders must prioritize protecting that data. Failing to do so can result in breaches of trust, legal consequences, and financial penalties. Implementing AI governance requires a commitment to integrity, ethical oversight, and ongoing learning to stay ahead of emerging challenges.

**Adaptability and Agility:**

If there's one thing AI teaches us, it's that adaptability is key. The modern business landscape changes fast, and leaders who aren't agile risk being left behind. AI can help leaders stay nimble by providing real-time insights into market trends, customer preferences, and potential disruptions.

**AI as a Strategic Compass**

AI can act like a strategic compass for leaders, helping them assess and modify their direction based on real-time data. For instance, AI-powered analytics can quickly detect shifts in consumer behavior, allowing leaders to adjust their product offerings or marketing strategies on the fly. The ability to pivot quickly separates successful companies from those flounder during disruptions.Take the retail industry during the COVID-19 pandemic as an example. The sudden shift to e-commerce caught many traditional retailers off guard. Still, companies that utilized AI to predict supply chain issues and adapt to changing consumer habits managed to stay afloat. AI gave them the agility to respond to a crisis quickly and efficiently.

**Algorithmic Bias**

# Transforming Business with AI

Artificial Intelligence (AI) promises a world of efficiency and innovation, but it also carries the risk of algorithmic bias—systematic and unfair discrimination that arises from the very data and models driving AI systems. While hiring algorithms have garnered significant attention for perpetuating biases, the issue is far-reaching, affecting areas such as facial recognition, credit risk assessments, and predictive policing.

**Real-World Examples of Algorithmic Bias**

*Facial Recognition Systems:* Studies by researchers such as Joy Buolamwini and Timnit Gebru have highlighted that many facial recognition algorithms exhibit significant racial and gender biases. For instance, these systems often misidentify individuals with darker skin tones and women at much higher rates than white males. Such inaccuracies have led to wrongful arrests, particularly in law enforcement applications, raising critical ethical and legal concerns.

*Credit Risk Assessments:* Financial institutions increasingly use AI to assess creditworthiness, but these systems can inherit biases from historical data. A notable example is the Apple Card controversy, where male applicants were reportedly granted higher credit limits than female applicants, despite similar financial circumstances. This sparked debates about transparency and fairness in financial AI applications.

*Predictive Policing:* Predictive policing systems, which use historical crime data to anticipate future criminal activity, have been criticized for disproportionately targeting minority communities. These biases stem from historically over-policed areas being overrepresented in training datasets, leading to a feedback loop that reinforces existing inequalities.

Dr. Yashwant Aditya

**Root Causes of Algorithmic Bias**

Algorithmic bias often originates from several interconnected factors:

*Biased Training Data:* AI systems learn from historical data, which may contain entrenched societal biases. For example, if past hiring decisions favored certain demographics, an AI model trained on such data will likely replicate those preferences.

*Homogeneity in Development Teams:* A lack of diversity among the teams designing and deploying AI systems can lead to blind spots, where biases are either overlooked or unintentionally embedded.

Systemic Societal Inequalities: AI mirrors the world it is trained on. If the training data reflects unequal systems, AI will likely perpetuate those inequalities.

**Mitigating Algorithmic Bias**

Businesses can adopt several strategies to identify, measure, and mitigate algorithmic bias:

*Diverse and Inclusive Datasets:* Organizations should strive to use datasets that represent a wide range of demographics. This involves actively seeking out underrepresented groups and ensuring their inclusion in training data.

*Algorithm Auditing:* Regular audits can help detect and address biases in AI systems. Third-party audits can provide an impartial review, ensuring fairness and accountability.

*Bias Testing Tools:* Tools like IBM's AI Fairness 360 and Google's What-If Tool enable developers to test for bias in their models and adjust algorithms accordingly.

*Diverse Development Teams:* A more inclusive AI workforce can bring varied perspectives to the table, reducing the likelihood of blind spots and fostering ethical AI design.

*Transparency and Explainability:* Businesses must ensure that AI decision-making processes are transparent and explainable. Leaders and end-users should be able to understand how decisions are made, enabling accountability and trust.

## Data Privacy

AI's reliance on vast amounts of data raises profound ethical concerns around privacy. Personal and sensitive data, if mishandled, can lead to breaches of trust, legal repercussions, and financial penalties. Protecting data privacy is not just a regulatory requirement; it is a cornerstone of ethical AI use.

### Ethical Challenges in Data Privacy

*Data Collection Practices:* Many AI systems collect extensive personal data without clear consent. For instance, mobile applications and online platforms often gather location, browsing history, and even biometric information, frequently without users' full awareness or understanding.

*Data Misuse and Overreach:* Collected data is sometimes repurposed in ways users did not consent to, as seen in the Cambridge Analytica scandal. This misuse not only undermines user trust but also highlights the need for stronger ethical safeguards.

# Dr. Yashwant Aditya

*Data Security Risks:* Large-scale data breaches, such as those experienced by Equifax and Marriott, demonstrate the vulnerabilities in data storage and protection. When AI systems rely on compromised data, they can amplify risks rather than mitigate them.

## Case Studies Highlighting Data Privacy Risks

*Cambridge Analytica:* This high-profile scandal exposed how personal data from millions of Facebook users was harvested without proper consent and used to influence elections. It underscored the ethical and regulatory gaps in data governance for AI-driven analytics.

*GDPR Fines:* The General Data Protection Regulation (GDPR) has led to significant fines for companies failing to protect user data. For instance, British Airways faced a $230 million fine for a data breach affecting over 400,000 customers. These penalties emphasize the importance of robust data protection practices.

## Strategies for Ethical Data Privacy Practices

*Differential Privacy:* Businesses can adopt differential privacy techniques, which add statistical noise to datasets, ensuring individual identities are protected while preserving data utility for AI analysis. This approach balances data privacy and functionality.

*Anonymization:* Data anonymization involves removing personally identifiable information (PII) from datasets, making it nearly impossible to trace data back to individuals. However, businesses must ensure that anonymization processes are robust to prevent re-identification attacks.

Informed Consent: Organizations should prioritize obtaining clear and explicit user consent for data collection. This involves transparent communication about how data will be used, stored, and shared.

*Data Minimization:* Collect only the data necessary for AI applications. Limiting data collection reduces the risk of misuse and demonstrates a commitment to ethical practices.

*Regulatory Compliance:* Adherence to laws like GDPR, the California Consumer Privacy Act (CCPA), and other regional regulations ensures a baseline level of data protection. Businesses should proactively monitor changes in regulatory landscapes to maintain compliance.

**Developing Governance Models**

As AI continues to shape industries, businesses must adopt comprehensive governance models to ensure its ethical use. Governance involves not just setting guidelines but fostering a culture of accountability and transparency within organizations. Below are actionable steps businesses can take to implement robust ethical AI practices:

## 1. Establish a Dedicated AI Ethics Board

A dedicated ethics board can oversee AI development and deployment within the organization. This board should consist of a mix of professionals, including:

- Technical experts to assess algorithmic performance and detect potential biases.
- Ethics specialists to ensure that AI aligns with societal and organizational values.
- Legal advisors to ensure compliance with local and international

regulations.

The board's primary responsibilities would include reviewing AI projects, ensuring alignment with ethical policies, and addressing any unforeseen ethical dilemmas. For instance, Google's short-lived AI ethics board highlighted the importance of diverse representation and organizational commitment to success.

## 2. Conduct Regular Audits for Ethical Compliance

Auditing AI systems is essential to ensure that they operate within ethical and legal boundaries. This includes:

*Bias Testing:* Analyzing predictions for discriminatory patterns and ensuring fairness across demographic groups.

*Performance Monitoring:* Regularly evaluating the accuracy and reliability of AI models.

*Privacy Compliance:* Verifying adherence to data protection laws, such as GDPR and CCPA. Regular audits provide an opportunity to catch and address issues before they escalate into public controversies or legal violations.

## 3. Develop Organization-Wide AI Ethics Policies

Ethical governance begins with clear, organization-wide policies. These should outline principles for AI development, deployment, and usage. Key elements of such policies include:

*Data Usage Guidelines:* Specify acceptable methods for collecting, storing, and processing data.

*Accountability Measures:* Define who is responsible for AI outcomes, ensuring human oversight remains integral.

*Stakeholder Engagement:* Encourage collaboration between developers, users, and affected parties to identify and mitigate risks.

For example, Microsoft has implemented AI ethics guidelines emphasizing inclusiveness, reliability, and transparency, serving as a blueprint for other organizations.

**Responsible AI Guidelines**

Adopting responsible AI practices requires businesses to align with existing ethical frameworks. Several globally recognized guidelines offer practical steps for building ethical AI systems.

## 1. EU's Ethics Guidelines for Trustworthy AI

The European Union's Ethics Guidelines for Trustworthy AI emphasize three pillars: lawfulness, ethics, and robustness. These guidelines are underpinned by seven core requirements:

**Human Agency and Oversight:** AI must empower humans, with safeguards to prevent harmful autonomy.

**Technical Robustness and Safety:** Ensure AI systems are resilient to errors and cyber threats.

**Transparency:** Promote explainability, so stakeholders understand how AI makes decisions.

**Diversity, Non-Discrimination, and Fairness:** Address biases and ensure inclusivity.

**Societal and Environmental Well-Being:** Develop AI that benefits society while minimizing environmental impact.

**Accountability:** Establish mechanisms for auditing AI systems and addressing grievances.

**Practical Steps for Businesses:**

- Implement tools that provide explainability, ensuring users understand AI outputs.
- Develop training programs to educate employees on trustworthy AI principles.
- Set up grievance mechanisms for users to report ethical concerns related to AI.

## 2. IEEE's Ethically Aligned Design

The IEEE's framework provides guidance on embedding ethics into AI system design, emphasizing:

- Transparency: Use open algorithms to foster trust.
- Privacy: Safeguard user data with robust encryption and anonymization techniques.
- Accountability: Ensure that human oversight remains central to AI decisions.

**Practical Steps for Businesses:**

- Adopt algorithm transparency by documenting decision-making processes.
- Establish privacy-preserving protocols like differential privacy to

secure sensitive information.

- Encourage cross-disciplinary collaboration to anticipate and mitigate ethical risks.

## 3. Montreal Declaration for a Responsible AI

- This framework focuses on the social impact of AI, advocating for systems that respect autonomy, equality, and justice. Its principles include:
- Well-Being: Prioritize human welfare over profit-driven motives.
- Equity: Ensure AI benefits are distributed fairly across society.
- Accountability: Maintain mechanisms for redress in case of ethical lapses.

**Practical Steps for Businesses:**

- Develop AI models with a user-centric approach, focusing on inclusivity.
- Allocate resources to monitor and address long-term societal impacts of AI.
- Set measurable benchmarks to track ethical performance over time.

**Implementing Responsible AI Guidelines**

To translate these frameworks into actionable steps, businesses can:

- Prioritize Explainability in AI Models Explainability ensures that AI decisions can be understood by non-technical stakeholders. Businesses can achieve this by:

- Using interpretable machine learning models like decision trees or linear regression for critical applications.
- Providing clear visualizations or explanations of AI predictions, enabling end-users to trust and validate outcomes.
- **Promote Fairness Across AI Outputs** Fairness requires that AI systems deliver equitable results across all demographics. Practical measures include:
- Designing algorithms that actively counteract historical biases in datasets.
- Testing outputs across diverse user groups to identify potential disparities.
- Using fairness-enhancing tools, such as Google's TensorFlow Fairness Indicators, to monitor and rectify discrepancies.
- Ensure Accountability Through Oversight Mechanisms Accountability mechanisms ensure businesses take responsibility for AI outcomes. This involves:
- Mandating human-in-the-loop (HITL) systems, where humans have the final say in critical decisions.
- Establishing clear accountability structures, with defined roles and responsibilities for ethical governance.
- Engage in Ethical Impact Assessments Before deploying AI, businesses should conduct ethical impact assessments to evaluate potential societal and environmental risks. These assessments involve:

**Predicting potential misuse of AI systems.**

- Assessing the environmental impact of energy-intensive AI training processes.
- Soliciting feedback from affected communities to ensure alignment with their needs and values.

## Addressing Adaptability and Ongoing Challenges

The ethical landscape of artificial intelligence (AI) is not static. With new technologies emerging at a breakneck pace, businesses and policymakers must remain vigilant, adaptive, and forward-thinking to navigate evolving challenges. This section explores the complexities of ethical dilemmas in dynamic environments and the need for accountability in real-time AI decision-making.

### Ethical Dilemmas in Dynamic Environments

AI technologies, such as generative AI and deepfakes, have introduced unprecedented ethical challenges. These innovations blur the line between creativity and manipulation, raising concerns about misinformation, security, and accountability.

### *1. The Emergence of Generative AI*

Generative AI models, such as OpenAI's GPT and DALL·E, can create human-like text, images, and even videos. While these tools have transformative potential, they also present ethical risks, including:

*Misinformation Proliferation:* Generative AI has been used to spread false information, creating realistic but fabricated news articles or social media posts. For example, during election cycles, AI-generated content has fueled political propaganda and deepened societal polarization.

*Copyright Violations:* Artists and content creators have raised concerns about AI models trained on copyrighted materials without permission, undermining intellectual property rights.

Addressing the Challenge:

*AI Content Watermarking:* Tech companies should embed watermarks or metadata in AI-generated content, making it easier to distinguish from human-created material.

*Ethical AI Use Policies:* Businesses adopting generative AI should establish clear guidelines that discourage its misuse for unethical purposes.

*Collaborative Governance:* Industry leaders, policymakers, and academics must collaborate to create frameworks that address the societal impact of generative AI technologies.

## 2. The Rise of Deepfakes

Deepfake technology uses AI to manipulate images and videos, often making it appear as though individuals said or did things they never did. While this technology can entertain or educate, its misuse has led to severe ethical concerns:

*Reputation Damage:* Deepfakes have been weaponized for character assassination, with public figures and private citizens alike becoming victims.

*Fraud and Security Threats:* Cybercriminals have used deepfake technology to impersonate executives, authorizing fraudulent transactions or extracting sensitive information.

**Mitigating the Risk:**

*AI-Powered Deepfake Detection:* Developing and deploying tools to identify manipulated content in real time.

*Legislation Against Deepfake Misuse:* Governments must introduce laws that penalize the creation or distribution of malicious deepfakes.

*Public Awareness Campaigns:* Educating the public on identifying and verifying digital content can reduce the impact of deepfake misinformation.

## 3. The Importance of Adaptability

As the ethical challenges of AI evolve, organizations must cultivate adaptability to stay ahead. Adaptability begins with leadership and extends across the entire organization. Key strategies include:

*Ongoing Training for Leadership:* Executives and managers must receive continuous training on emerging AI technologies and associated ethical risks. For instance, workshops on the implications of generative AI can equip leaders to make informed decisions.

*Fostering a Culture of Awareness:* Employees at all levels should be encouraged to report ethical concerns, creating a proactive environment for addressing new challenges.

*Scenario Planning:* Organizations should engage in scenario-based planning to anticipate and mitigate the risks posed by emerging technologies.

# Dr. Yashwant Aditya

### Real-Time AI Decision-Making

AI's ability to make instant decisions in dynamic environments has revolutionized industries. However, the ethical implications of such decisions are significant, especially in areas like dynamic pricing and predictive policing.

## 1. Dynamic Pricing

Dynamic pricing algorithms adjust prices in real time based on supply, demand, and customer behavior. While this practice can optimize revenue, it raises ethical questions about fairness and transparency.

### Key Ethical Concerns:

*Price Discrimination:* Algorithms may unfairly charge different prices based on a customer's location, browsing history, or perceived willingness to pay. For instance, ride-sharing apps have faced backlash for surge pricing during emergencies, leading to accusations of exploitation.

*Exacerbating Inequality:* Dynamic pricing can disproportionately impact low-income individuals, making essential goods and services less accessible.

### Strategies for Ethical Implementation:

*Transparency in Pricing Models:* Businesses should disclose how dynamic pricing works, building trust with customers.

*Caps on Surge Pricing:* Setting limits on price increases during emergencies can prevent perceived exploitation.

*Fairness Audits:* Regularly evaluating dynamic pricing algorithms ensures

150

they do not perpetuate or amplify social inequalities.

## 2. Predictive Policing

Predictive policing uses AI to analyze historical crime data and forecast potential criminal activity. While it promises to enhance public safety, it also poses significant ethical risks.

*Key Ethical Concerns:*

Reinforcing Bias: Predictive policing algorithms often rely on biased historical data, disproportionately targeting marginalized communities. For example, studies have shown that such systems can unfairly label specific neighborhoods as high-crime areas, perpetuating systemic discrimination.

*Erosion of Privacy:* Predictive policing often involves mass surveillance, raising concerns about individual rights and freedoms.

Strategies for Ethical Implementation:

*Human Oversight:* Decisions based on predictive policing should involve human review to prevent unjust actions.

*Community Involvement:* Engaging affected communities in the development and evaluation of predictive policing programs can foster trust and accountability.

*Data Scrutiny:* Policymakers should ensure that training datasets are diverse, representative, and free from historical biases.

**The Need for Human Oversight**

While AI excels at processing vast amounts of data and making rapid

Dr. Yashwant Aditya

decisions, its lack of human intuition and moral reasoning necessitates oversight. Human oversight is critical for:

*Contingency Planning:* Humans can intervene when AI systems produce unexpected or harmful outcomes. For example, if a financial AI system mistakenly triggers a market crash, human operators can step in to stabilize the situation.

*Ethical Judgments:* Decisions involving moral or cultural nuances—such as sentencing recommendations in criminal justice—require human empathy and contextual understanding.

**Best Practices for Human Oversight:**

*Human-in-the-Loop (HITL) Systems:* Incorporating humans at key decision points ensures accountability and prevents blind reliance on AI.

*Redundancy Mechanisms:* Establishing fallback procedures for critical AI applications minimizes risks in case of system failure.

*Continuous Monitoring:* Real-time monitoring of AI systems helps detect and rectify issues as they arise.

**Building Resilience in Ethical AI**

Addressing adaptability and ongoing challenges requires organizations to build resilience into their AI strategies. Key elements of a resilient AI framework include:

Investing in Ethical Research: Organizations should fund research into the societal impact of AI technologies, contributing to a deeper understanding of ethical challenges.

Collaborating with External Stakeholders: Partnerships with academia, nonprofits, and regulatory bodies can help businesses stay ahead of ethical developments.

Learning from Failures: When ethical lapses occur, organizations should conduct post-mortem analyses to identify root causes and implement corrective measures.

By embracing adaptability, fostering human oversight, and addressing the challenges of real-time decision-making, businesses can navigate the ethical complexities of AI in an ever-changing landscape.

## Ethical AI in Collaboration and Strategic Design

The integration of artificial intelligence (AI) into collaboration and strategic planning offers immense potential to revolutionize industries. However, these advancements come with significant ethical considerations. This section examines how human-AI synergy can be optimized for creativity and ethical decision-making, and explores the role of leadership in using AI responsibly for strategic purposes.

### Collaborative AI Design

AI is increasingly being used as a collaborative partner rather than just a tool, enhancing creativity and efficiency across various fields. However, ensuring ethical boundaries are maintained is critical to fostering trust and fairness in such collaborations.

### 1. Human-AI Synergy in Creativity

AI has demonstrated remarkable potential in supporting creative endeavors, from generating art to designing products. When AI complements human creativity, the results can be groundbreaking.

**Examples of Collaborative Success:**

*Art and Design:* AI tools like Adobe Sensei and DeepArt allow artists to generate ideas, refine designs, and explore styles that might not have been possible otherwise. For instance, fashion designers use AI to analyze trends and predict future preferences, resulting in innovative collections.

*Writing and Content Creation:* AI models like GPT can draft content or suggest edits, speeding up the creative process. For example, screenwriters have used AI to brainstorm plot ideas or improve dialogue, enhancing storytelling efficiency.

*Product Innovation:* Companies like Autodesk use generative design AI to optimize engineering solutions. AI generates thousands of potential designs based on specified parameters, enabling engineers to select the most effective and sustainable option.

**Key Ethical Considerations:**

*Transparency in Attribution:* It is crucial to clearly distinguish between AI-generated and human-created elements, ensuring proper credit and avoiding deception.

*Respecting Intellectual Property (IP):* AI models must not infringe on copyrighted works during training or content generation. A notable controversy arose when an AI art competition winner was accused of using copyrighted material without acknowledgment.

**Strategies for Ethical AI-Assisted Creativity:**

Implement Licensing Agreements: Use licensed datasets to train AI models, ensuring artists and creators are fairly compensated.

*Develop Ethical AI Guidelines:* Organizations should define boundaries for AI usage, including safeguards against plagiarism.

*Educate Users:* Provide training for users to understand the limitations and responsibilities of AI tools.

## 2. Navigating Ethical Boundaries in Creativity

While collaborative AI design can amplify innovation, it must operate within ethical norms. Unchecked AI-assisted creativity risks:

*Plagiarism:* AI models might inadvertently replicate existing works due to biased training data. For instance, an AI-generated song could mimic copyrighted music without intention, sparking legal disputes.

*Cultural Appropriation:* AI might misinterpret cultural elements, using them out of context or inappropriately in designs or narratives.

Preventive Measures:

*Curated Training Data:* Ensure AI systems are trained on diverse and culturally sensitive datasets to avoid perpetuating stereotypes or biases.

*Pre-Release Reviews:* Conduct ethical reviews of AI-generated content before public release to ensure compliance with IP laws and cultural norms.

By addressing these challenges, businesses can use AI to support human creativity while fostering ethical practices.

**Ethical Leadership in Strategic AI Use**

Leaders play a pivotal role in integrating AI into long-term strategic planning while upholding ethical principles. Effective leadership ensures that AI applications align with organizational values and broader societal interests.

## 1. The Role of Leaders in Ethical AI Integration

Leaders must approach AI adoption with a balanced perspective, leveraging its capabilities without compromising ethical standards.

**Key Leadership Responsibilities:**

*Informed Decision-Making:* Leaders must understand AI's limitations and risks to make informed choices about its applications. For instance, they should weigh the benefits of predictive analytics against potential data privacy concerns.

*Promoting Transparency:* Ethical leaders ensure that AI-driven decisions are explainable, fostering trust among stakeholders. This is particularly crucial in sectors like healthcare or finance, where opaque algorithms can have life-altering consequences.

**Examples of Ethical Leadership:**

*Healthcare Innovations:* Organizations like IBM Watson Health use AI to assist in diagnosing diseases and recommending treatments. Ethical leadership ensures that such systems prioritize patient safety and consent.

*Retail and Marketing:* Companies like Amazon use AI for personalized recommendations. Ethical leadership involves mitigating risks like algorithmic discrimination or manipulative marketing practices.

## 2. Avoiding Over-Reliance on AI

While AI can provide valuable insights, over-reliance on it can lead to ethical pitfalls, including:

*Ignoring Societal Impacts:* Blindly following AI-generated insights may overlook broader social consequences. For example, an AI system optimizing warehouse logistics might recommend policies that strain worker well-being.

*Loss of Accountability:* Organizations that defer entirely to AI risk eroding human accountability for critical decisions.

**Strategies to Counter Over-Reliance:**

*Human-AI Collaboration:* Encourage human oversight and intervention in AI-driven decisions to ensure ethical considerations are addressed.

*Scenario-Based Decision-Making:* Use AI insights as one of several inputs in strategic planning, combining them with human intuition and ethical judgment.

*Stakeholder Engagement*: Involve diverse stakeholders—employees, customers, and community representatives—in evaluating AI strategies.

## 3. Long-Term Ethical Strategy

Leaders must adopt a forward-looking approach to integrate AI into organizational strategies while preparing for future ethical challenges.

**Components of a Long-Term Strategy:**

*Developing Ethical AI Roadmaps:* Leaders should create roadmaps that outline ethical AI objectives, including milestones for compliance, transparency, and fairness.

*Investment in R&D:* Investing in research ensures that organizations stay ahead of emerging ethical dilemmas, such as those posed by generative AI or quantum computing.

*Fostering Ethical Culture:* Ethical leadership involves instilling values throughout the organization, ensuring that every employee recognizes their role in responsible AI use.

**Case Studies: Successful Ethical AI Integration**

1. **Google's AI Principles:** Google developed a comprehensive framework for ethical AI, emphasizing fairness, accountability, and social benefit. One notable success is their policy to avoid AI applications that could cause harm, such as weaponized AI.

2. **Microsoft's Responsible AI Strategy:** Microsoft established an AI, Ethics, and Effects in Engineering and Research (AETHER) committee to oversee AI applications. This initiative has resulted in ethical innovations, such as inclusive AI tools that enhance accessibility for people with disabilities.

3. **Salesforce's Ethical Use Advisory Council:** Salesforce created an advisory council to evaluate the ethical implications of its AI products. This body reviews potential risks and ensures AI applications align with the company's values.

**Practical Steps for Organizations**

To ensure ethical AI practices, businesses need to integrate responsibility into their AI development lifecycle. The following checklist outlines key steps to guide organizations in achieving this goal.

## 1. Stakeholder Involvement in AI Development

Engaging diverse stakeholders ensures that AI systems are built with inclusivity and fairness in mind.

*Internal Stakeholders:*

Involve cross-functional teams, including developers, ethicists, legal advisors, and domain experts, in decision-making processes.

Ensure leadership is educated on AI's ethical implications to provide informed oversight.

*External Stakeholders:*

Collaborate with external experts, such as academics and non-governmental organizations, for unbiased input.

Include end-users and community representatives in consultations to understand the potential societal impacts of AI systems.

*Actionable Tip:* Host workshops or focus groups with stakeholders to gather feedback during AI design and testing phases.

## 2. Continuous Monitoring for Unintended Consequences

AI systems must be regularly audited to identify and mitigate unintended consequences, such as bias or operational risks.

*Define Metrics for Ethical Performance:*

Dr. Yashwant Aditya

- Use fairness, accountability, and transparency as benchmarks for evaluating AI systems.
- Track the accuracy and consistency of AI decisions over time.

**Establish Feedback Loops:**

- Create mechanisms for users to report errors or concerns regarding AI systems.
- Use real-world data to refine algorithms and reduce bias.

Example: Financial institutions deploying AI for credit scoring should regularly evaluate whether their algorithms unintentionally discriminate against specific demographics.

## 3. Transparent Reporting on AI Usage

Transparency builds trust with stakeholders and ensures accountability in AI operations.

*Publicly Share AI Policies:*

Publish ethical guidelines outlining how AI is developed and used.

Include information on data sources, algorithms, and decision-making processes.

*Adopt Explainable AI:*

Design systems that can provide clear, human-understandable explanations for their outputs.

Offer customers and regulators insight into how decisions, such as loan approvals, are made.

*Actionable Tip:* Use transparency reports similar to those published by Google, which detail progress and challenges in ethical AI development.

**Case Studies and Best Practices**

Several organizations have set benchmarks in ethical AI implementation. The following examples highlight how these companies have integrated responsible practices into their AI strategies.

## 1. Google's AI Principles

In 2018, Google introduced a comprehensive set of AI principles to ensure that its AI systems are socially beneficial and ethically sound.

**Key Features of Google's AI Principles:**

Avoid Harm: Google prohibits the use of its AI in applications that could cause harm, such as weaponized systems.

Incorporate Privacy Protections: By embedding privacy-preserving technologies into AI, Google ensures data security and user trust.

Promote Fairness: Google emphasizes reducing bias by using diverse datasets and continually auditing its systems.

Impact: These principles have guided Google's development of AI products like TensorFlow Privacy, which allows developers to create machine learning models that adhere to differential privacy standards.

## 2. Microsoft's AI for Good Initiative

Microsoft has spearheaded several initiatives to align AI applications with global ethical standards.

**Core Strategies in Microsoft's Approach:**

Inclusive Design: Microsoft prioritizes accessibility, developing AI tools such as Seeing AI, which assists visually impaired individuals by narrating their surroundings.

Ethical Oversight: The company established the AETHER (AI, Ethics, and Effects in Engineering and Research) Committee to oversee ethical AI implementation.

Transparency Tools: Microsoft created tools like InterpretML, which enable explainability in AI models and support developers in understanding decision-making processes.

Impact: These efforts have set an industry standard, positioning Microsoft as a leader in responsible AI use.

## 3. Salesforce's Ethical AI Framework

Salesforce's approach to ethical AI focuses on creating systems that prioritize fairness and societal benefit.

**Key Practices:**

Ethical Use Advisory Council: Salesforce established an advisory body to evaluate the ethical implications of its AI tools, such as Einstein, which provides predictive analytics for businesses.

Customer Empowerment: Salesforce gives customers control over their AI settings, allowing them to choose how data is used in predictions and insights.

Bias Detection: The company integrates bias detection tools into its platforms to reduce discrimination in AI outputs.

Impact: This framework has enhanced trust among Salesforce's customers and partners, showcasing the value of embedding ethical considerations into AI systems.

**Challenges in Implementation**

While the steps and case studies above provide a strong foundation, organizations face challenges in implementing ethical AI, including:

Balancing Innovation with Regulation: Striking a balance between rapid AI development and compliance with emerging ethical standards can be complex.

Resource Constraints: Smaller organizations may lack the resources to establish ethics boards or conduct extensive audits.

Evolving Ethical Norms: As AI technologies advance, ethical considerations must continually adapt to new scenarios, such as the rise of generative AI.

Solutions:

Collaborative Networks: Partnering with industry groups, such as the Partnership on AI, can help organizations share resources and expertise.

Scalable Solutions: Start with simple, scalable initiatives, such as adopting open-source tools for fairness and bias detection.

Dr. Yashwant Aditya

## Case Study:

## Nike's Use of AI in Collaborative Design

To see AI as a collaborative partner, let's look at how Nike has harnessed AI to push the boundaries of product design and customer experience.

### Background

Nike, a global leader in sportswear, faced the challenge of staying competitive in a rapidly changing retail landscape. Consumers increasingly demanded personalized products, faster production times, and more sustainable practices. Nike needed a way to meet these expectations while maintaining their brand's innovative edge.

### AI in Product Customization and Design

To tackle these challenges, Nike turned to AI to help streamline their product design and customization processes. Through a combination of AI-driven customer data analysis and machine learning, Nike was able to offer personalized product recommendations and design options that aligned with individual preferences.

For example, Nike's "Nike By You" service allows customers to customize shoes by selecting colors, materials, and other features. Behind the scenes, AI analyzes past customer choices, market trends, and feedback to suggest unique and likely popular designs.

This allows Nike to provide a highly personalized experience while adhering to market trends.

In addition, AI-driven design tools helped Nike's product teams. AI algorithms could analyze athletes' vast amounts of performance data, determining the most effective materials and designs for enhancing performance. Designers could then use these insights to refine their concepts, ultimately leading to innovative products that performed better and were more aligned with consumer needs.

**AI in Supply Chain and Sustainability**

Beyond just design, Nike also used AI to improve sustainability and optimize its supply chain. Through AI-powered analytics, Nike could predict demand more accurately, reducing excess inventory and waste. AI also played a role in optimizing the production process, helping the company achieve its sustainability goals by minimizing material usage and reducing carbon emissions.

**Results and Benefits**

The results of Nike's AI collaboration have been impressive. By leveraging AI as a collaborative partner, Nike improved its ability to deliver products that resonated with customers while reducing production timelines and enhancing sustainability. The partnership between AI and Nike's design teams has led to faster innovation cycles, more personalized customer experiences, and greater efficiency in their operations.

Moreover, Nike has used AI to drive their sustainability efforts. The data-driven insights have allowed them to identify areas where waste could be reduced, whether through optimizing the supply chain or improving the efficiency of production materials. This has helped Nike maintain its position as an industry leader in design, performance, and corporate responsibility.

**Lessons from Nike**

The key takeaway from Nike's experience is that AI isn't a replacement for human creativity or leadership. Instead, it's a powerful tool that enhances these qualities. By collaborating with AI, Nike's teams could focus more on innovation, creativity, and long-term strategy, while AI handled the more time-consuming tasks like data analysis and trend prediction. This kind of partnership allows companies to stay competitive in rapidly changing markets without sacrificing the quality of their products or their commitment to sustainability.

**Building Teams Around AI Collaboration**

As AI continues to evolve, building teams that can collaborate with AI will become increasingly important. Leaders must create environments where AI is seen as a valuable tool rather than a competitor. This involves upskilling employees, teaching them how to work alongside AI systems, and fostering a culture of innovation.

It's essential to recognize that collaboration between humans and AI requires a shift in mindset. People need to understand that AI is there to support their work, not replace it. The most successful organizations will be those that encourage collaboration between AI and their workforce, creating a synergy that drives innovation and efficiency.

**The Future of Leadership with AI**

AI is transforming leadership in profound ways. From ethical governance to adaptability in strategy and collaborative design, AI offers new possibilities that can elevate leadership to new heights. But with these possibilities come challenges, particularly in ethics and governance. Leaders must navigate the integration of AI thoughtfully, ensuring that their systems are transparent, accountable, and fair.

The key takeaway here is that AI isn't just a trend—it's a tool that will continue to shape the future of leadership. Those who embrace AI, understand its potential and address its challenges head-on will be better equipped to lead their organizations into the future.

But AI alone isn't enough. Leaders must still bring their human qualities—intuition, empathy, and ethics—to the table. The best leaders of tomorrow will be those who can strike the right balance between AI and human intelligence, unlocking new possibilities in governance and strategy that we're only just beginning to explore.

Dr. Yashwant Aditya

## Exercise

### 1. What is one key ethical challenge when using AI in leadership and decision-making?

A) AI always leads to accurate decisions
B) AI can perpetuate inequalities if the data is biased or incomplete
C) AI is free of human bias
D) AI systems never require governance

**Answer:** B) AI can perpetuate inequalities if the data is biased or incomplete

### 2. Which of the following is NOT part of establishing an AI governance framework?

A) Ensuring transparency in AI decision-making
B) Prioritizing data privacy and security
C) Allowing AI systems to make decisions without human input
D) Setting ethical guidelines for data usage

**Answer:** C) Allowing AI systems to make decisions without human input

### 3. What is the primary role of AI in leadership and strategy?

A) AI replaces human leaders
B) AI acts as a strategic compass, helping leaders adapt quickly to changes
C) AI makes final decisions without human intervention
D) AI is only used for automating routine tasks

**Answer:** B) AI acts as a strategic compass, helping leaders adapt quickly to changes

### 4. Which of these industries has seen the impact of AI in

**adapting quickly during a crisis?**

A) Retail
B) Aerospace
C) Pharmaceuticals
D) Oil and Gas

**Answer:** A) Retail

**5. What does "algorithmic bias" refer to?**

A) AI that makes decisions randomly
B) AI that only processes neutral data
C) AI that is trained with biased data, leading to unfair decisions
D) AI that always supports equality

**Answer:** C) AI that is trained with biased data, leading to unfair decisions

**6. True or False: Algorithmic bias is only a problem in hiring algorithms.**

**Answer:** False. Algorithmic bias affects various fields, including facial recognition, credit risk assessments, and predictive policing.

**7. What is one method to mitigate algorithmic bias?**

A) Reducing the diversity of training data
B) Performing regular algorithm audits
C) Avoiding any form of transparency
D) Using only historical data

**Answer:** B) Performing regular algorithm audits

**8. How does the homogeneity of AI development teams**

Dr. Yashwant Aditya

**contribute to algorithmic bias?**

A) It ensures that all perspectives are considered
B) It may overlook or unintentionally embed biases
C) It leads to AI systems that are unbiased
D) It helps reduce the transparency of AI decisions

**Answer:** B) It may overlook or unintentionally embed biases

**9. True or False: Data privacy concerns related to AI primarily involve issues of user consent and data security.**

**Answer:** True. Data privacy concerns include user consent and the security of personal data.

**10. What was the key ethical issue in the Cambridge Analytica scandal?**

A) The AI algorithm was too transparent
B) Users' data was harvested without proper consent and misused
C) AI was used to predict consumer behavior
D) Data security measures were overly stringent

**Answer:** B) Users' data was harvested without proper consent and misused

**11. What is an essential aspect of AI decision-making that leaders must understand?**

A) The decision-making process should be fully automated
B) AI decisions should always be unexplainable
C) AI decisions must be traceable to data and logic
D) AI should make decisions in complete isolation from human input
**Answer:** C) AI decisions must be traceable to data and logic

## 12. True or False: Leaders have no responsibility to ensure AI systems are ethical.

**Answer:** False. Leaders must take responsibility for ensuring AI systems are ethical and aligned with standards of fairness, transparency, and accountability.

# Chapter 8:
# Real-World AI Implementation
# Strategies

## Strategy: Setting the Stage for Success

When it comes to implementing artificial intelligence (AI) in your business, having a solid strategy is like having a well-drawn map—it directs your efforts and resources to the places where they'll yield the most benefit. While AI has the potential to revolutionize industries and unlock new opportunities, it's also fraught with potential risks. If you jump in without a plan, you could end up wasting both time and money, or worse, implementing a system that doesn't align with your business needs.

### ADD INFOGRAPHIC ON REAL WORLD
### IMPLEMENTATION STRATEGIES USING AI

A clear AI implementation strategy ensures you are maximizing return on investment (ROI) and minimizing risks. It helps you focus on what's most important—whether that's enhancing customer service, optimizing supply chains, or personalizing marketing efforts. The key here is to see AI not just as a tool but as a means to an end. What do you want to achieve? Answering this question is critical before diving into any AI project. Without a well-defined goal, even the most powerful AI won't deliver value.

Let's not forget, AI implementation isn't a one-time effort. It's a journey of ongoing learning, adaptation, and optimization. This is where the value of a phased approach comes into play. By rolling out AI initiatives in phases, businesses can experiment with smaller projects, learn from them, and then scale up with confidence. For instance, rather than overhauling an entire customer service department with AI chatbots overnight, a business can start by automating responses for simple customer queries. As the AI proves successful and gains trust within the organization, more complex tasks can be added.

Another benefit of a phased approach is that it helps reduce risks. Instead of betting everything on a single large-scale AI project, businesses can make incremental investments, gauge their performance, and make informed adjustments along the way. Think of it like driving in fog: you can only see a little bit ahead, so you move cautiously, assessing conditions as you go. In the same way, phasing your AI implementation allows for better decision-making at each stage.

The beauty of AI is that it learns and improves over time. Businesses must adopt this mindset too. By starting small, measuring success, and expanding gradually, companies ensure they're staying nimble in the face of inevitable challenges and market shifts.

Dr. Yashwant Aditya

## Aligning AI with Business Goals

One of the biggest mistakes companies make when implementing AI is treating it like a shiny new toy rather than a tool that needs to align with specific business objectives. Without clear alignment, you may end up with impressive AI capabilities that don't actually serve your core goals, leading to wasted resources and unmet expectations.

To avoid this pitfall, start by taking a step back and identifying how AI can help solve real business challenges. What pain points can it address? What processes need improvement? This involves not only leadership but also engaging teams on the ground to understand where AI can deliver the most value. Is it in customer service, where AI can reduce wait times and handle repetitive inquiries? Or perhaps in operations, where AI can help predict supply chain disruptions?

Once you've identified the areas where AI can be most effective, you'll need to evaluate whether your business has the necessary skills and expertise to support the implementation. Often, businesses have internal teams with domain expertise but lack AI-specific skills. This is where training or hiring external AI specialists can come into play. It's important to bridge these skills gap early in the process so that you have people who can guide the AI system from development to deployment, ensuring that it's well integrated into your current operations.

Furthermore, evaluating your technological infrastructure is crucial. AI solutions require substantial computing power and often need to integrate with existing systems such as customer relationship management (CRM) software, enterprise resource planning (ERP) systems, or marketing platforms. Before jumping into AI implementation, ask yourself: Does your current tech stack support AI deployment? Is it scalable? You might need to upgrade your infrastructure to accommodate AI's computational and data needs, which can be expensive but essential to long-term success.

Take inventory of what you already have in place. Many businesses don't realize that they're sitting on a goldmine of data and technological resources that can be leveraged for AI. However, this data needs to be in a usable form. Clean, well-structured, and accessible data is the backbone of any successful AI project. AI models are only as good as the data they're trained on, so this preparation stage is vital.

A good starting point could be conducting a technology audit. This allows you to assess what systems are already compatible with AI tools and what may need to be updated or replaced. For example, if your data storage is decentralized or your existing software doesn't support API integrations with AI solutions, you'll face bottlenecks down the road. By ensuring your technological infrastructure is AI-ready from the beginning, you can save significant headaches later.

It's also important to have a clear timeline and key performance indicators (KPIs) that align with your broader business goals. For instance, if your goal is to reduce customer churn through personalized marketing, then KPIs might include reduced churn rates, improved customer satisfaction, or increased sales from repeat customers. Aligning AI with these specific business outcomes keeps the project focused and makes it easier to measure success.

Remember, AI should be a part of your long-term business strategy, not a quick-fix solution. By thoughtfully aligning AI initiatives with your business goals, you ensure that AI is working for you—not the other way around.

# Case Studies

## IBM Watson and MD Anderson Cancer Center

*A High-Tech Misstep*
*What went wrong?*

MD Anderson Cancer Center, one of the biggest names in cancer treatment, teamed up with IBM's Watson, aiming to change the game in healthcare. The idea? Use AI to sift through mountains of patient data and help doctors make smarter, faster decisions about treatment. It sounded like a match made in heaven—technology and medicine working hand-in-hand. But after five years and a jaw-dropping $62 Million down the drain, the plug was pulled.

**The hiccup?**

As impressive as Watson's brain power was, it was biting off more than it could chew. Cancer treatment isn't a one-size-fits-all solution; it requires a human touch, the kind of careful judgment that doctors bring to the table. Watson, for all its smarts, couldn't quite keep up with the fast-paced, high-stakes environment of MD Anderson. It struggled to churn out real-time advice that doctors could actually use in the heat of the moment. Add to that the fact that it didn't gel well with MD Anderson's systems and workflows, and you've got a recipe for disaster. In short, Watson was brilliant but out of its depth in this particular setting.

## The takeaway?

AI is a tool, not a magic wand. It's like handing someone a Ferrari without showing them how to drive it—bound to end in disaster. MD Anderson's expensive misstep shows that AI needs to work with you, not just for you. Especially in fields like healthcare, where lives are on the line, tech has to play nicely with the professionals who know the ropes. AI can help, but it shouldn't try to run the show.

## Hertz and Accenture

*When Digital Dreams Turn into Nightmares*
*What happened?*

Hertz, the car rental giant, hired Accenture, a big-shot consulting firm, to overhaul its digital platforms. With $32 million on the table, the plan was to build a slick new website and mobile app that would make renting a car as easy as hailing an Uber. But instead of a high-tech triumph, Hertz found itself facing a nightmare, and they ended up suing Accenture for botching the job.

**Where did it all go south?**

Accenture's grand design was full of bugs, glitches, and missing features. The app didn't work smoothly across devices, and many of Hertz's must-have features were MIA. What should've been a revolutionary customer experience turned into a frustrating mess. Accenture's vision and Hertz's needs were miles apart, and the project came crashing down.

**Lesson learned?**

AI can't fix everything if the basics aren't in place. You can't slap some fancy tech onto a shaky foundation and hope it'll work. It's like putting icing on a burnt cake—it's still a disaster underneath. Hertz's tech fiasco shows that if AI isn't built with a clear understanding of what the business actually needs, it's just money down the drain.

**Target and Predictive Analytics:**

**Hitting the Bullseye**

**What happened?**

Unlike some of the AI misfires, Target hit a home run with its AI-driven predictive analytics. By tracking customers' buying habits, Target's system started predicting life events like pregnancy before customers even knew what hit them. Subtle changes in shopping carts—like unscented lotions and vitamins—signaled to Target that a baby was on the way, and they started sending personalized offers for baby products before the parents-to-be even asked.

**Why did it work so well?**

Target nailed it because their AI system was perfectly aligned with their goal: getting closer to their customers and boosting sales. They weren't just throwing AI at a problem and hoping for the best. They had a clear vision of what they wanted to achieve—loyalty and sales—and the AI system was designed with those goals in mind.

**Lesson learned?**

When you know where you're aiming, AI can help you hit the bullseye. Target's success story shows that if you line up your AI efforts with clear, practical business goals, the results can be pure gold. It's not about jumping on the AI bandwagon—it's about using it in a way that makes sense for your business.

## Amazon and AI in Recruitment

*A Biased Blunder*

*What went wrong?*

Amazon, always at the forefront of tech, decided to build an AI tool to help with recruitment, hoping to speed up the hiring process. But instead of saving time and effort, the AI became infamous for reinforcing gender biases. The algorithm had been trained on resumes submitted over a decade, most of which came from men, particularly in technical roles. As a result, the system started favoring men and downgrading resumes with words like "women's," as in "women's soccer team."

**The root of the problem?**

The AI system was learning from a biased set of data, so naturally, it produced biased results. It wasn't in sync with Amazon's diversity goals, and instead of leveling the playing field, it tipped the scales even further in the wrong direction.

**Lesson learned?**

AI is only as good as the data it learns from. It's like cooking a meal with spoiled ingredients—no matter how fancy the recipe, the dish is going to taste off. Amazon's stumble highlights the importance of ethical AI development. You can't just focus on efficiency; you've got to make sure the technology doesn't end up working against your values.

## Netflix and Recommendation Algorithms

*Streaming Success*

*What happened?*

Netflix has become a household name, and a lot of that success can be chalked up to its AI-powered recommendation engine. The system learns what you like by analyzing your viewing habits, and it gets smarter the more you watch. That's how it keeps you hooked, offering up just the right shows and movies at the right time. The more you watch, the better the recommendations get—it's a win-win.

### The secret sauce?

Netflix's AI works so well because it's tightly aligned with the company's main objective: keeping users engaged. By making sure you're always one click away from something you want to watch, Netflix reduces the chances of you canceling your subscription. They're not just using AI for the sake of it—they're using it to serve a clear business goal.

### Lesson learned?

When AI and business goals are in perfect harmony, magic happens. Netflix's recommendation engine shows that when AI is used strategically, it can be a massive driver of success. It's not about the tech—it's about how you use it.

### Zara and AI in Inventory Management:

*A Seamless Fit*

*What happened?*

Zara, the fast-fashion giant, relies on speed and precision to stay ahead in a cutthroat industry. To keep up with constantly changing trends, they turned to AI to help manage inventory and predict demand. Their AI system analyzes store data to figure out which items will be hot and ensures that those items are always in stock, minimizing waste and maximizing profits.

**Why did it work?**

Zara's AI system fits like a glove with their business model. The company's goals of cutting costs, reducing waste, and keeping shelves stocked with trendy items all align perfectly with what the AI system is designed to do. It's this kind of fine-tuning that has kept Zara ahead of the competition.

**Lesson learned?**

When AI is used to solve the right problems, it can work wonders. Zara's experience shows that AI can streamline operations and boost profitability, but only when it's purpose-built to fit the company's unique needs.

Dr. Yashwant Aditya

**The Right Approach:**

**Developing a Framework for Success**

Choosing the right AI approach for your business can feel overwhelming at first. With so many different types of AI technologies and models to choose from, it's crucial to develop a clear framework that will guide your decisions. Not every AI tool is going to be the right fit for your business, and selecting the wrong one can lead to poor performance, wasted investment, and unmet expectations. To avoid these issues, businesses need to take a systematic approach that starts with their specific goals and available data.

The first step in developing this framework is understanding your business's unique needs and the data you have available. Different AI technologies excel at different tasks, so your selection should be driven by what you want to achieve. For example, if your goal is to enhance customer service by automating responses to simple queries, a natural language processing (NLP) model might be the best fit. On the other hand, if you need to forecast product demand and optimize your supply chain, predictive analytics powered by machine learning (ML) could be the way to go.

Before choosing an AI tool, it's essential to consider the type and quality of data available. AI relies heavily on data, and its effectiveness depends on having a sufficient volume of high-quality, relevant data to train the algorithms. Without this, even the most sophisticated AI models will produce subpar results. Businesses need to audit their data to ensure it's clean, accurate, and comprehensive enough to meet the AI's needs.

Once you've clarified your business goals and assessed your data, the next step is selecting the most appropriate AI approach. This might involve using off-the-shelf AI solutions, developing custom models, or even collaborating with external AI vendors. Off-the-shelf solutions are often easier to implement and can be a good starting point, especially for smaller businesses with limited AI expertise. These pre-built solutions are designed for specific tasks—like chatbots, recommendation engines, or image recognition—so they can provide immediate value with minimal customization.

However, if your business has more complex needs or operates in a highly specialized industry, developing custom AI models may be the better choice. This route allows for more flexibility and the potential to build AI systems that are deeply integrated into your workflows. For instance, a custom AI solution could be developed to optimize your manufacturing processes, factoring in variables that are unique to your operations, such as machine wear and tear or specific supply chain constraints. The downside is that custom models typically require more time, resources, and specialized knowledge to develop.

Dr. Yashwant Aditya

Another factor to consider when choosing the right approach is how scalable the AI solution is. Scalability is critical for long-term success, as your business needs and data volumes will likely grow over time. A solution that works well today might not be suitable in a year if it doesn't scale with your business. When evaluating AI tools, ask yourself: Can this solution handle larger datasets as we grow? Does it have the flexibility to adapt as our goals evolve? Scalability is often built into AI models, but it's worth ensuring that any solution you select can expand with your business's future needs.

Collaboration with external AI vendors can be another effective strategy, especially for companies that lack the in-house expertise to build and maintain AI systems. Vendors can provide pre-built models or help customize AI solutions for specific business needs. This option reduces the pressure on your internal teams and allows you to tap into the vendor's specialized knowledge. However, it's important to carefully evaluate potential partners, ensuring they have a proven track record and offer ongoing support for the implementation.

Finally, a crucial aspect of developing the right AI approach is flexibility. AI projects, by nature, are iterative processes. It's unlikely you'll get everything right on the first try, so your approach should allow for adjustments along the way. This is where pilot projects and testing become essential. Starting with small, manageable AI projects allows your team to assess whether the solution is meeting expectations and, if necessary, refine the approach before scaling up. These small projects act as learning opportunities, helping you understand what works, what doesn't, and how to best optimize AI for your business.

**The right AI approach isn't a one-size-fits-all solution. It requires thoughtful consideration of your business goals, available data, and the long-term scalability of the system. By developing a structured framework for selecting and implementing AI, you can ensure that the tools you adopt are aligned with your needs and have the flexibility to grow with your business.**

**Exercise: AI Implementation Strategy**

**This exercise will guide you through the process of implementing AI in your business, based on the strategies outlined in Chapter 8. Each section below includes prompts that require you to reflect on key considerations for AI implementation.**

**Part 1: Setting the Stage for Success**

1. **Assessing Your AI Readiness:** Think about your business. On a scale of 1-10 (1 being least ready and 10 being most ready), rate how ready your business is for AI implementation. Consider factors such as infrastructure, team expertise, and existing data resources.

**Reflection Prompt:**

- What factors contributed to your rating?
- What areas need the most improvement to make AI a feasible part of your business?

2. **Phased Implementation Approach:** Recall the analogy of driving in fog. How can you start small and incrementally implement AI in your organization? Identify one department or process that would benefit from a small-scale AI experiment.

**Activity:**

- **Choose a Department:** (e.g., Customer Service, Marketing, Operations)
- **Define the First Step:** (e.g., Automating responses to simple inquiries, Using AI-powered analytics to monitor trends)
- **Goal:** What is your objective for this phase? (e.g., Reduce response time, improve campaign targeting)

**Part 2: Aligning AI with Business Goals**

3. **Business Objectives Alignment:** AI should not be an isolated project but a tool for achieving specific business goals. Take a moment to reflect on your business goals. How can AI help achieve them?

**Exercise:**

- **Identify a Core Business Goal:** (e.g., Increase customer satisfaction, optimize supply chains)

- o **AI's Role:** How will AI support or drive this goal forward? (e.g., Personalized recommendations, predictive analytics)

4. **Bridging the Skills Gap:** AI is a powerful tool, but it requires expertise. Do you have the right internal resources or do you need to hire/train new talent?

**Activity:**

- o **Evaluate Your Team:** Does your current team have the technical expertise for AI? (Yes/No)
- o If not, list two actions you can take to bridge the gap. (e.g., Hire AI experts, Provide AI training to existing employees)

5. **Technological Infrastructure Readiness:** Review your business's current technological setup. Is it AI-ready? Identify the systems and tools that need to be upgraded or integrated to support AI.

**Task:**

- o **Create an Infrastructure Checklist:** List key elements of your current tech stack and evaluate their compatibility with AI.
  - Data storage (Centralized/Decentralized)
  - Existing software (CRM, ERP systems)
  - APIs for integration

Dr. Yashwant Aditya

## Part 3: Implementing AI in Real-World Scenarios

6. **Define KPIs for AI Implementation:** AI success is measured by results. Define clear KPIs that align with your business goals and will help you assess the effectiveness of AI.

**Interactive Task:**

- o **Choose a KPI for Your Business Goal:** (e.g., For customer service, it could be reducing average response time)
- o **Set a Target:** (e.g., Reduce response time by 30% within 6 months)

## Part 4: Analyzing Case Studies

7. **IBM Watson and MD Anderson Cancer Center:** Reflect on the case study mentioned in the chapter. What went wrong, and what could have been done differently?

**Activity:**

- o **List Key Challenges in the Case Study:**
  - Was there a clear goal for AI? (Yes/No)
  - Was the technology properly integrated into existing systems? (Yes/No)
  - Did they have the necessary expertise to deploy AI? (Yes/No)
- o **Propose Solutions:**
  - What could IBM Watson and MD Anderson have done differently to ensure a successful AI implementation?

190

## Conclusion: Building Your AI Strategy

8. **Wrap-Up:** After completing these exercises, summarize your AI strategy in one sentence.

**Final Reflection:**

- o **What's the most important thing you learned about AI implementation?**

# Chapter 9:
# The Future of Business

In today's world, business is changing at lightning speed, and artificial intelligence (AI) is at the heart of that transformation. From automating routine tasks to generating insights that would take a human mind day, maybe even weeks, AI is shaking things up in ways that we could have only dreamed of a few decades ago. Gone are the days of AI being reserved for tech giants and sci-fi fantasies—now, it's in the hands of businesses of all sizes, helping them leap ahead of the competition.

Imagine a world where your business can predict what your customers want before they even know it themselves. Where data doesn't just sit there in endless spreadsheets but comes to life, guiding decisions, identifying trends, and pointing out problems before they happen. That's the power of AI, and it's already here, transforming the way we do business. If you're not embracing it, well, you're being left in the dust.

AI is no longer a "nice-to-have" but a necessity to stay competitive. Companies that jump on board now are finding themselves ahead of the curve, while those that resist will eventually face the harsh reality that staying in the past is no longer an option. But it's not just about staying in the game—it's about leading it. The businesses that embrace AI have the chance to become the trailblazers of their industries.

Let's take a deep dive into what it means to build an intelligent business model in the age of AI, how you can start implementing AI into your own business, and why now is the time to act.

**The Intelligent Business Model**

**Defining the Intelligent Business Model**

First things first—what is an Intelligent Business Model? Well, think of it like this: in the traditional business model, you rely on human intuition, spreadsheets, and historical data to make decisions. But an Intelligent Business Model adds AI into the mix, and suddenly, you have a partner that's crunching numbers, analyzing trends, and spotting opportunities in real time.

In an Intelligent Business Model, AI doesn't just support decision-making—it drives it. AI allows businesses to adapt faster, making decisions based on real-time data rather than waiting for trends to reveal themselves over time. It's like having a supercharged brain, one that works 24/7, never gets tired, and never overlooks the small stuff. It's not just smart; it's intelligent.

One standout example is Netflix. By analyzing the viewing habits of millions of users, Netflix uses AI to recommend shows and movies, predict future content preferences, and even decide which new projects to greenlight. It's this kind of intelligent decision-making that has kept them at the forefront of the streaming world, even as competitors have flooded the market.

Amazon is another classic case. With AI-driven algorithms, Amazon can predict customer needs, optimize supply chains, and create personalized shopping experiences. The company's AI systems even monitor warehouse conditions and predict equipment failures before they happen, keeping everything running smoothly. In both cases, AI isn't just a tool; it's the backbone of the entire business model.

**Building Your Intelligent Business Model**

So, how do you build an Intelligent Business Model? It starts with recognizing the opportunities. AI can touch nearly every aspect of a business, from customer service to supply chain management to marketing. But you don't have to go all in at once. The smartest businesses start by identifying specific areas where AI can provide the most value.

Start with the low-hanging fruit—those tedious, repetitive tasks that take up valuable time and energy. AI thrives on these. Whether it's automating customer inquiries through chatbots, managing inventory, or analyzing sales data, you'll see an immediate return on your investment. But remember, this is just the beginning.

Once you've successfully implemented AI in one area, expand.

Develop a roadmap for transitioning the rest of your business processes to an intelligent model. This includes integrating AI with your existing technology stack, training your teams to leverage AI-powered tools, and establishing a culture that's ready to innovate.

Data is key in an Intelligent Business Model, and AI lives and breathes data. The more data you feed it, the smarter and more efficient it becomes. Whether you're tracking customer interactions, monitoring market trends, or managing internal processes, AI will help you find patterns you never even knew existed. The best part? AI continues to learn and evolve, so as your business grows, your AI gets smarter, too.

**Recap: Key Takeaways**

Now, let's recap some of the key insights we've explored throughout this book.

*AI is transforming businesses:* The shift from traditional to AI-powered business models is happening faster than ever. Those who embrace AI are positioning themselves for success, while those who don't are falling behind.

*AI drives decision-making:* Businesses that integrate AI into their processes can make decisions based on real-time data, adapt faster to market changes, and deliver more personalized experiences to their customers.

*Automation is a game-changer:* By automating repetitive tasks, businesses free up human capital to focus on more strategic, creative endeavors, driving innovation and growth.

*AI is accessible to businesses of all sizes:* Whether you're a small startup or a global enterprise, AI has become more affordable and scalable. The tools are there—you just need to start using them.

Of course, every silver lining has a cloud, and there are common concerns surrounding AI implementation. One major concern is the fear of job displacement. While it's true that some jobs will be automated, the rise of AI is also creating new opportunities. Think of AI as a tool to complement human workers, not replace them. The future workforce will need to adapt, learning how to work alongside AI rather than in competition with it.

Another concern is data security. With more data being collected and analyzed, businesses need to ensure they're protecting sensitive information. Luckily, AI can also be used to bolster cybersecurity efforts, detecting threats and vulnerabilities faster than traditional systems.

Lastly, there's the worry that AI implementation is too complex or expensive for smaller businesses. But the reality is that AI has never been more accessible. Many cloud-based platforms now offer AI-as-a-service, allowing businesses to scale their use of AI without investing in expensive infrastructure.

Overall, the benefits of AI far outweigh the challenges, especially for businesses of all sizes. With the right strategy, any company can start reaping the rewards of AI implementation.

**The Call to Action: So, What Are You Waiting For?**

We've spent this whole book talking about the future of business, but here's the thing—it's already here. AI isn't just something to think about down the line—it's happening now, and the businesses that are taking action are already seeing results. So, what are you waiting for?

The first step is to start small. Implement AI in one area of your business and see how it goes. Test it, tweak it, and learn from the process. The beauty of AI is that it's constantly evolving, so there's always room to improve. Don't feel like you have to get it perfect on the first try—just get started.

There are a wealth of resources and tools available to support your AI journey. From online courses to AI consulting services, you can find guidance at every step. Platforms like Google Cloud, Microsoft Azure, and AWS offer AI tools that are scalable and affordable. Many of these tools don't require a deep understanding of coding or data science, making AI accessible to anyone with the right mindset.

And here's where the real challenge comes in—dare to lead. Don't just follow the AI trend; become a leader in your industry. This is your chance to not only keep up with the competition but to set the pace for others to follow. As AI continues to evolve, the businesses that are on the cutting edge will be the ones reaping the most significant rewards.

Whether it's using AI to enhance customer experiences, streamline operations, or develop entirely new products and services, the possibilities are endless. And the best part? We're just scratching the surface of what AI can do.

**Conclusion**

The future of business isn't something that's going to arrive in 10 or 20 years—it's unfolding right in front of us. AI is the key to unlocking new levels of efficiency, insight, and creativity, and those who embrace it will find themselves at the forefront of their industries. But the time to act is now. The competition isn't waiting, and neither should you.

So, let this be your call to action: seize the moment, leverage AI to its fullest, and build your business's future today. Remember, the only limit to what AI can achieve is your imagination and your willingness to innovate. The tools are out there, and the future is yours for the taking.

**Exercise**

**Quiz: The Future of Business - AI and the Intelligent Business Model**

1. **What is the key advantage of integrating AI into business models?**
   o  A) It replaces human workers entirely.
   o  B) It enhances decision-making by analyzing real-time data.
   o  C) It reduces the need for customer service.
   o  D) It allows businesses to operate without human input.

2. **Which of the following companies is highlighted as an example of successfully using AI for decision-making?**
   o  A) Google
   o  B) Netflix
   o  C) Microsoft
   o  D) Apple

3. **In the context of AI, what is meant by the "Intelligent Business Model"?**
   o  A) A business model that focuses on minimizing the use of technology.
   o  B) A business model where decisions are made based on real-time data and AI-driven insights.
   o  C) A business model that relies solely on human intuition and spreadsheets.
   o  D) A business model that ignores AI and relies only on historical data.

4. **What is one of the first areas businesses should focus on when implementing AI?**
   o  A) Marketing strategy

- o B) Low-hanging fruit—tedious and repetitive tasks
- o C) Financial investments
- o D) Corporate culture

5. **How does Netflix use AI to maintain its competitive edge?**
   - o A) By recommending shows and movies based on user habits.
   - o B) By controlling pricing and subscription models.
   - o C) By using AI to run its customer service operations.
   - o D) By designing and producing movies automatically.

6. **What is a major benefit of implementing AI in supply chain management, as seen with companies like Amazon?**
   - o A) Predicting customer needs and optimizing inventory.
   - o B) Automating customer support inquiries.
   - o C) Reducing the need for employees in warehouses.
   - o D) Avoiding the use of any physical stores.

7. **What role does data play in an Intelligent Business Model?**
   - o A) It is optional but can be helpful.
   - o B) Data is irrelevant, as decisions are made based on intuition.
   - o C) AI needs data to operate and make smarter decisions over time.
   - o D) Data is only necessary for marketing and sales strategies.

8. **What should businesses do once they've successfully implemented AI in one area?**
   - o A) Completely overhaul the business.

- o   B) Expand AI integration to other areas gradually.
- o   C) Stop using AI altogether.
- o   D) Avoid training teams to use AI tools.

9.  **Why is the integration of AI not just a one-time effort for businesses?**
    - o   A) AI cannot adapt to new challenges after implementation.
    - o   B) AI continues to learn, evolve, and improve as the business grows.
    - o   C) AI can only be used for specific tasks.
    - o   D) AI implementation is temporary and doesn't require follow-up.

10. **According to the chapter, what is a significant risk for businesses that resist adopting AI?**
    - o   A) They will quickly become industry leaders.
    - o   B) They will continue thriving without needing AI.
    - o   C) They will eventually fall behind competitors who embrace AI.
    - o   D) They will avoid technology disruptions and maintain stability.

Dr. Yashwant Aditya

**Answers:**

1. **B)** It enhances decision-making by analyzing real-time data.
2. **B)** Netflix
3. **B)** A business model where decisions are made based on real-time data and AI-driven insights.
4. **B)** Low-hanging fruit—tedious and repetitive tasks
5. **A)** By recommending shows and movies based on user habits.
6. **A)** Predicting customer needs and optimizing inventory.
7. **C)** AI needs data to operate and make smarter decisions over time.
8. **B)** Expand AI integration to other areas gradually.
9. **B)** AI continues to learn, evolve, and improve as the business grows.
10. **C)** They will eventually fall behind competitors who embrace AI.

# About the Author

Yashwant Aditya is a trailblazing technology expert and thought leader with over a decade of experience at the intersection of network security, cybersecurity, and artificial intelligence. Recently completed Masters in AI for Business at the prestigious University of Oxford, Yashwant combines academic rigor with hands-on expertise to craft innovative solutions for today's most pressing technological challenges. Holding a PhD in Artificial Intelligence and Cybersecurity, as well as another Master's degree in Cybersecurity and Management from the University of Warwick, UK, Yashwant has built a career rooted in both deep technical knowledge and strategic foresight. As a Senior Network Security Consultant at Lenovo, he spearheads critical projects in network infrastructure deployment, risk assessment, and change management. His technical repertoire spans cutting edge domains like machine learning, large language models (LLMs), deep learning, and vulnerability management. Yashwant's passion for continuous learning is reflected in his impressive collection of certifications, including CISM, CISSP, AWS Cloud Practitioner, and Azure Administrator Associate. A graduate of the Future Leaders Programme at NUS, he pairs his technical acumen with refined leadership skills to inspire teams and drive impactful results. An accomplished researcher and author, Yashwant has published

Dr. Yashwant Aditya

extensively on topics such as VPN frameworks and energy-efficient cryptographic processors in esteemed journals like Telematique and NeuroQuantology. His contributions have also been showcased at global conferences like the IEEE International Conference on AI in Cybersecurity. Not content with just advancing theory, Yashwant has co-developed innovative technologies such as an AI powered personal and business financial advisor, securing his place as an inventor as well as a scholar. Beyond his professional accolades, Yashwant is deeply committed to mentoring aspiring technologists and fostering global conversations on cybersecurity and AI. Through this book, he aims to demystify complex technologies and empower readers to harness their potential for entrepreneurial success. When not immersed in technology or writing, he enjoys exploring new ideas that bridge the gap between innovation and practical application. With a career spanning role at industry giants like PCCW, Wipro InfoTech, and GIC Singapore, Yashwant brings a wealth of diverse experiences to his writing. His unique perspective makes 208 Transforming Business with AI this book an essential guide for anyone seeking to navigate the rapidly evolving landscape of AI entrepreneurship. Yashwant welcomes connections and discussions with readers. You can reach him at yashwant.aditya@hotmail.com to share your thoughts, ask questions, or explore potential collaborations in the exciting world of AI and cybersecurity.

www.ingramcontent.com/pod-product-compliance
Lightning Source LLC
Chambersburg PA
CBHW061020220326
41597CB00016BB/1728